The
CHEW
A Year of Celebrations

ALSO AVAILABLE FROM *THE CHEW*

The *New York Times* Best-selling books:
The Chew: Food. Life. Fun.
The Chew: What's for Dinner?

The
CHEW

A Year of Celebrations
FESTIVE AND DELICIOUS RECIPES FOR EVERY OCCASION

Edited by Ashley Archer and Jessica Dorfman Jones

KINGSWELL

NEW YORK • LOS ANGELES

The
CH

PAGE 1: Mini Baked Alaska, recipe on page 184.

PAGE 2: Roasted Pork Loin with Cranberries, recipe on page 96.

PAGE 7, TOP: Chicken Wings, recipe on page 20.

PAGE 7, BOTTOM: Bananas Foster Crepes, recipe on page 152.

PAGE 8: Grilled Butterflied Leg of Lamb with Mint Pesto, recipe on page 138, and Braised Scallions and Potatoes, recipe on page 140.

PAGE 11: Citrus Upside-Down Cake, recipe on page 226.

Content coordinator: Kerry McConnell
Food photographer: Andrew Scrivani
Food stylists: Jackie Rothong, Ian McNulty,
    Lauren Palmeri, Devan Dror
Prop stylist: Francine Matalon-Degni
Crafter: Tom Tamborello
Craft photographer: Andrew Scrivani
Hand model: Lauren Palmeri

The Chew: A Year of Celebrations—Photographer Credits:
Lou Rocco/ABC: 4–5, 9, 17, 23, 28, 61, 62, 71, 77, 80, 94, 98, 104, 135, 137, 140, 143, 144–145, 149, 196, 205, 208, 213, 221, 240, 242–243, 244, back cover image; Jeffrey Neira/ABC: 11, 12–13, 19, 21, 22, 24–25, 52–53, 64, 68–69, 91, 93, 121, 126–127, 131, 163, 164–165, 170, 215, 235; Lorenzo Bevilaqua/ABC: 50, 56, 88, 100–101, 111, 118, 119, 154, 156, 175, 183, 189, 231, 236; Donna Svennevik/ABC: 36–37, 39, 41, 84–85, 108, 124, 190, 195, 246; Ida Mae Astute/ABC: 95, 224; Fred Lee/ABC: 167; Host headshots by Craig Sjodin/ABC

For more information address Kingswell, 125 West End Avenue, New York, NY 10023

Editorial Director: Wendy Lefkon
Executive Editor: Laura Hopper
Editor: Jessica Ward
Designer: Gregory Wakabayashi

ISBN 978-1-4847-1108-8

Printed in the United States of America

FIRST EDITION
10 9 8 7 6 5 4 3 2 1

V381-8386-5-14220

SUSTAINABLE FORESTRY INITIATIVE
Certified Chain of Custody
At Least 20% Certified Forest Content
www.sfiprogram.org
SFI-00993

For Text Only

ACKNOWLEDGMENTS

All right, time to come clean. Despite the fact we have five hosts who know more about cooking than a canary knows about cats, the demands of producing a five-day-a-week cooking show are formidable. From the very beginning, our stars have relied on a wonderful team of young men and women who are the food heart of *The Chew*. Their kitchen is about twenty feet from the set, tucked away behind the staging equipment, oozing delicious smells and creative fervor from the early morning hours.

After each show, our hosts talk to Ashley Archer, the senior producer about what they want to cook the following day. Ashley then takes the recipe to her team of kitchen Jedi, Kevin Mendlin, Hugh Jernigan, Jackie Rothong, Lauren Palmeri, Ian McNulty, and Devan Dror, who then begin to put the food side of the show together.

It is their job to make sure every recipe is tested, priced, and then artfully presented for still shots and beauties—long before we even warm up the studio lights.

All restaurants live or die by the speed and efficiency of the line cook. All cooking shows live or die by the skill and speed of their culinary team. They set the pace, fire the imagination, create beauty for the audience, and make sure every ingredient is exactly where it needs to be at exactly the right time.

The skill, fun, and confidence of our hosts are supported by the very same vibes coming from the kitchen. So before we do publish one more page let me say thank you. I love what you do, and so do all our viewers.

—**Gordon Elliott**, *Executive Producer*

CONTENTS

INTRODUCTION

A couple of years ago I watched Clinton Kelly explain why he loved to entertain and celebrate so much. "I love my friends and family, but I feel like we never have the time to just hang out anymore, we are all so busy. So when I do see them I want to show how much I care by all the little things I do to prepare the meal."

I watched Michael, Mario, Carla, Daphne, and the studio audience smile in recognition of this truth. We all understood it's our very personal, very personalized gift to people we care for. No matter the event, we are really celebrating our friendships.

So when it came time to make a new book, we wanted to show you some beautiful dishes that will knock your loved ones' socks off but not leave you a joyless stress case by the end of the meal. These are the easiest, tastiest, most spectacular celebratory meals our five fabulous hosts have in their repertoires.

We hope it will inspire you to turn a meal into a celebration.

—Gordon Elliott, *Executive Producer*

ALL-AMERICAN CLASSICS

We're lucky enough to have several holidays and traditions that are uniquely American and supremely fun. And associated with delicious food, of course. What could be more American than celebrating holidays that remind us how our nation was built, and big-game days that bring us together despite our differing team loyalties? Here at *The Chew* we've created so many memorable traditions and recipes that perfectly reflect these all-American festivities that we decided to put them all together and share them as a group. Eat, drink, and be very, very merry!

GAME DAY

Slam Dunk Punch

Serves: **12 to 14**   Skill Level: **Easy**   Prep Time: **5 minutes**   Inactive Cook Time: **10 to 15 minutes**

Many sports fans prefer to drink beer during the big game, but once they've tried this point-scoring punch, they'll be singing its praises all the way to the end zone! This punch takes the basic principles of a tequila sunrise (tequila and orange juice) and makes them special by bringing the orange flavor into the picture three different ways.

½ gallon orange sherbet

6 ounces frozen orange juice concentrate, optional

2 liters ginger ale

2 cups tequila

1 cup orange liqueur

Orange slices, for garnish

1. Place the sherbet and frozen orange juice concentrate in a punch bowl. Allow to thaw for 10 to 15 minutes.

2. Stir in the ginger ale, tequila, and orange liqueur.

3. Garnish with orange slices and serve.

CLINTON
By the way, it's not pronounced "sher-BERT," it's "sher-BET." Trust me, it's fancier that way!

Potato Nachos

Serves: **6 to 8**   Skill Level: **Easy**   Prep Time: **25 minutes**   Cook Time: **20 to 25 minutes**

Why stick with tortilla chips when you're making nachos? Who says you can't experiment? What's stopping you from getting a little inventive? Nothing! To make these nachos, we replace classic tortilla chips with homemade potato chips and then upgrade the cheese situation by replacing cheddar with blue cheese. These nachos are just as crunchy, cheesy, messy, and addictive as ever, but with a little sophisticated twist. Cocktail party food, anyone?

FOR THE POTATOES:

3 quarts vegetable oil

3 Idaho potatoes

Salt, to taste

FOR THE BLUE CHEESE DIP:

2 tablespoons butter

2 tablespoons flour

1¼ cups milk, heated

1 cup blue cheese, crumbled

Salt and pepper, to taste

2 scallions, thinly sliced

Pinch of chili flakes, optional

Malt vinegar, optional

TO MAKE THE POTATOES:

1. Heat the vegetable oil in a large heavy-bottomed pot to 325°F. It should come halfway up the sides of the pot.

2. Slice the potatoes thicker than an average potato chip, approximately a ¼-inch thick. Soak the potato slices in ice water to remove excess starch.

3. Take the slices out of the water, rinse, and dry on paper towels. Make sure they are dry before transferring to the oil.

4. Fry the sliced potatoes in small batches, cooking until fork-tender, about 8 minutes per batch. Remove from the oil with a strainer and set aside.

5. Turn the heat up under the oil until the temperature reaches 360°F.

6. Refry the potatoes until golden brown, crunchy on the edges, and slightly tender in the center; about 5 minutes per batch.

7. Using a strainer, remove from oil and place on a paper towel–lined plate. Season immediately with salt.

TO MAKE THE BLUE CHEESE DIP:

8. In a medium-sized pot, melt the butter and whisk in the flour. Cook for 3 to 4 minutes over medium heat until thick.

9. Ladle in the milk and keep whisking. Bring to a boil and then reduce the heat to simmer for 2 to 3 minutes, until creamy. Remove from heat.

10. Fold the blue cheese into the sauce and adjust seasoning with salt and pepper.

11. Garnish the dip with thinly sliced scallions, and chili flakes if desired. Serve with potato chips and malt vinegar.

NFL players or chili judges? Victor Cruz, Jesse Palmer, and Jerome Bettis tell *The Chew* crew how they like to chow down on game day.

It's a Wing Thing

Here are three great takes on wings, because let's face it . . . you can never have enough wings on game day. But you've gotta mix it up or your taste buds might get bored. Carla, Daphne, and Mario are bringing it with these distinct ideas on how to make your wings sing.

CARLA: If there's one food that shouts "Touchdown!" it's chicken wings. One of the great things about wings is that there are so many different ways to make them flavorful and unique; the possibilities are endless! Everyone can have his or her special recipe that becomes a signature dish. I love my Nashville, Tennessee–inspired hot wings. A little heat and a little sweet make them irresistible.

DAPHNE: Why mess with the original? Classic buffalo wings are right up my alley. They're easy to make (fewer than five ingredients!), they're fried (even if you're eating healthy you can always give yourself a treat), and they're just so darned delicious.

MARIO: The sauce for these wings is the ultimate in classic Filipino flavors. The basics of the Filipino pantry (fish sauce, soy sauce, cane sugar vinegar) are all here, along with the freshness of cilantro and the spice of chilies. All the contrasts in flavor are perfect and perfectly addictive.

Basic Wing Recipe

Serves: 8 to 10   Skill Level: **Easy**   Prep Time: **10 minutes**   Cook Time: **20 to 25 minutes**

FOR THE WINGS:

2 to 4 cups vegetable oil, for frying

3 pounds chicken wings

Salt and freshly ground black pepper, to taste

CARLA
If time is a factor, you can bake the wings the day before and fry them on the day of the party.

TO MAKE THE WINGS:

1. Preheat your oven to 350°F.

2. Place a large Dutch oven over medium-high heat and add vegetable oil. Using a deep-fry thermometer to monitor the temperature, heat the oil to 360°F.

3. Spread the wings out on a baking tray and season liberally with salt and pepper. Bake for 15 to 20 minutes, until just cooked through.

4. Remove from the oven and let cool slightly. In the meantime, prepare wing sauce of choice.

5. When your oil has reached 360°F add wings to oil and deep-fry until golden and crispy, working in batches, about 5 minutes per batch. Drain the fried wings on paper towel–lined plates and season them with salt.

6. Place the wings in a bowl and pour prepared sauce over the top, mixing to evenly coat all of the wings.

7. Serve the hot wings with your favorite accompaniments.

Along with regular guest cohost Curtis Stone, Clinton, Carla, Daphne, and Michael discuss their MVPs: Most Valuable Plates.

FOR CARLA'S SPICED OIL:

3 tablespoons vegetable oil

2 tablespoons cayenne pepper

1 teaspoon paprika

2 teaspoons red pepper flakes

2 teaspoons salt

½ teaspoon garlic powder

1 teaspoon sugar

FOR DAPHNE'S MAPLE BUFFALO SAUCE:

¼ cup maple syrup

1 cup hot sauce

½ cup butter

2 teaspoons salt

FOR MARIO'S ADOBO SAUCE:

2 tablespoons cane sugar vinegar

1 tablespoon coconut balsamic vinegar, optional

2 teaspoons fish sauce

2 tablespoons soy sauce

2 serrano chilies, chopped

1 bunch scallions, chopped

3 tablespoons brown sugar

¼ cup basil leaves, chopped

¼ cup cilantro leaves, chopped

MARIO
If you don't have cane sugar vinegar, you can instead mix honey and red wine vinegar.

TO MAKE CARLA'S SPICED OIL:

1. Heat oil in a small saucepan over medium heat until simmering.

2. Add the cayenne, paprika, red pepper flakes, salt, garlic powder, and sugar. Cook until fragrant, about 30 seconds.

3. Transfer to a large bowl and coat the hot, fried wings.

TO MAKE DAPHNE'S MAPLE BUFFALO SAUCE:

1. Combine the maple syrup, hot sauce, butter, and salt in a small saucepan.

2. Bring to a simmer and stir to melt the butter and combine the ingredients.

3. Transfer to a large bowl and coat the hot, fried wings.

TO MAKE MARIO'S ADOBO SAUCE:

1. Combine the vinegars, fish sauce, soy sauce, serrano peppers, scallions, brown sugar, basil, and cilantro, whisking together in a large bowl until fully combined.

2. Toss the wings to coat and serve.

Green Chili

Serves: **10**   Skill Level: **Easy**   Prep Time: **30 minutes**   Cook Time: **1 to 1½ hours**

When most people think of chili, they think of the classic mix of meat, beans, and spicy red sauce (shredded cheese and chopped onion optional). Well, think again. In New Mexico, when you order chili you've gotta be clear if you want red or green. If you go green, you're gonna get a version of this chili; it has no beans, but there's pork and green chilies galore. Red and green chilies are actually the same vegetable. The difference is when you pick them. Green means early and red means later; the green are milder and crazy delicious. Stop reading and start cooking!

3 tablespoons extra-virgin olive oil

2 pounds boneless pork shoulder, cut into one-inch cubes

Salt and pepper, to taste

1 yellow onion, chopped

3 garlic cloves, minced

3 fresh jalapeños, chopped

¼ cup fine white cornmeal

1, 28-ounce can San Marzano tomatoes, finely chopped with juices

1, 15-ounce can hominy, drained

2 cups hatch green chilies, roasted, peeled, and chopped

2 chipotle chilies in adobo, roughly chopped

3 cups chicken stock

½ cup cilantro, leaves picked, for garnish

1 lime, cut into wedges, for garnish

½ cup finely chopped white onion, for garnish

10 corn tortillas, to serve

1. Heat the olive oil over medium-high heat in a 4-quart Dutch oven with a cover.

2. Add the pork in small batches and season with salt and pepper. Cook until lightly browned, about 4 minutes, and then remove from the pan. Set aside.

3. Add the onion, garlic, and jalapeños to the Dutch oven and sauté for 3 minutes until soft and translucent. Add the fine cornmeal, and stir for 1 to 2 minutes. Once combined, add the tomatoes, hominy, green chilies, and chipotle chilies, stirring to incorporate the ingredients.

4. Add the chicken stock, then the seared pork. Lower the heat, and cover the pot. Simmer for 1 to 1½ hours, until the meat is tender.

5. Garnish with cilantro, lime, and finely chopped white onion. Serve with fresh corn tortillas.

Ten-Layer Bar

Serves: **12**   Skill Level: **Easy**   Prep Time: **30 minutes**   Cook Time: **8 to 10 minutes**
Inactive Cook Time: **1 hour**

Oscar Wilde, one of the most brilliant writers of all time, said, "Nothing succeeds like excess"; and we're not going to argue! So forget all other dessert bars that claim to be decadent with their three, seven, or eight layers. We're bringing out the big guns with this ten-layer bar. Chocolate, peanut butter, cookies, and chocolate-hazelnut spread are just the beginning. Are you ready for a countdown to a really Wilde bar? Ten layers . . . nine layers . . . eight layers . . .

2 cups graham cracker crumbs

½ cup melted butter

1 cup chocolate-hazelnut spread

2 cups toasted chopped pecans

2 cups crumbled vanilla wafer cookies

2 cups crumbled salted pretzels

1 cup chunky peanut butter

2 cups crumbled crispy chocolate chip cookies

14 ounces sweetened condensed milk

2 cups crushed potato chips

1 cup semisweet chocolate chips, melted

1. Preheat oven to 350°F. Grease a 9- x 13-inch baking dish.

2. In a food processor fitted with a blade, pulse the graham cracker crumbs and the butter until combined. Press the graham cracker mixture into the bottom of the greased pan. Bake the crust until golden brown, 8 to 10 minutes. Let cool.

3. Warm the chocolate-hazelnut spread for easy pouring. Drizzle over the crust and spread into an even layer. Sprinkle pecans evenly over the chocolate-hazelnut spread.

4. Continue with remaining ingredients, ending with the potato chips, evenly distributing to create defined layers. Finish by drizzling melted semisweet chocolate over the crushed potato chips.

5. Place in the refrigerator to chill for 1 hour. Cut into 1½- x 3-inch bars.

DAPHNE
When you're adding a sauce or spread to a recipe, it really helps to put it in a heat-resistant glass jar and heat it in a pot of hot water, or even throw it in the microwave. Then it's so easy to pour!

Chocolate Walnut Cookies

Serves: **24**   Skill Level: **Easy**   Prep Time: **10 minutes**   Cook Time: **7 to 8 minutes**

Inactive Cook Time: **30 minutes**

Sometimes when it comes to sweets, the simplest recipes are the best. These cookies are easy to make, classically delicious, and therefore absurdly comforting, particularly with a glass of cold milk. The addition of a little bit of cinnamon to the recipe beautifully offsets the walnuts and brown sugar; don't be surprised if you're sneaking to the kitchen late at night for just one more before bed!

2 1/4 cups all-purpose flour

1/4 teaspoon baking soda

1/4 teaspoon salt

1/2 teaspoon ground cinnamon

8 ounces cold, unsalted butter, divided

3/4 cup granulated sugar

3/4 cup light brown sugar

2 large eggs

1 teaspoon vanilla extract

2 cups mini chocolate chips

2 cups walnuts, toasted and roughly chopped

1. Preheat the oven to 350°F and line a sheet pan with parchment paper.

2. Combine the flour, baking soda, salt, and cinnamon in a small bowl and whisk together. Set aside.

3. Melt 2 ounces of butter in a microwaveable dish. Set aside.

4. Cut remaining butter into tablespoon-sized pieces. In the bowl of a standing mixer, cream butter and both sugars until the butter is incorporated. Do not overmix!

5. Add in the eggs and vanilla, and mix until incorporated. With the mixer on low speed, add in the melted butter, then gradually add the flour mixture. Stir in the chocolate chips and walnuts.

6. Place the dough in a 1-gallon zip-top bag and roll out into an even square, about an inch thick. Refrigerate the dough until firm, about 30 minutes.

7. Remove the dough from the plastic bag and cut the dough into 1-inch squares. Place the pieces two inches apart on a parchment-lined baking sheet.

8. Bake for 7 to 8 minutes or until the cookies are slightly brown around the edges. Cool slightly on a rack. Serve warm.

CARLA

If you're going to a potluck and have permission to use the oven, don't bother baking cookies at home. Just take your dough to the party, throw those cookies in the oven, and serve up a warm treat!

FOURTH OF JULY

Kentucky Buck

Serves: 1   Skill Level: **Easy**   Prep Time: **5 minutes**   Cook Time: **10 minutes**

What do you do when you want a grown-up drink but you can't drink? Or you just don't have any hooch in the house? You go on ahead and make a mocktail like my Kentucky Buck. The secret to a great mocktail is to let it stand on its own as a delicious drink but still be recognizable as a take on the original. In this case, it's a bourbon cocktail. With a few magic ingredients and a little alchemy, you'll swear you're ready for Independence Day.

FOR THE SIMPLE SYRUP:

1 cup granulated sugar

1 cup water

FOR THE KENTUCKY BUCK:

2 ounces simple syrup

½ teaspoon cayenne pepper, plus more to taste

3 strawberries, divided

1 ounce lemon juice

2 dashes Angostura bitters

Ginger beer, to top off

TO MAKE THE SIMPLE SYRUP:

1. Place the sugar and the water in a small saucepan and bring to a boil. Cook until the sugar has dissolved, about 5 minutes. Cool and store in an airtight container for up to two weeks. Makes 1 cup simple syrup.

TO MAKE THE KENTUCKY BUCK:

2. In a drink shaker, mix the simple syrup and cayenne pepper (plus more to taste).

3. In the bottom of a mixing glass, muddle 2 of the strawberries with lemon juice.

4. Add muddled strawberries and bitters to drink shaker, and shake with ice.

5. Strain over glass filled with ice and top off with ginger beer. Garnish with remaining strawberry.

CARLA

This drink is very versatile. Just swap out the fruit depending on the season, and you can customize it for any occasion! Try it with blackberries, cranberries, raspberries . . . the possibilities are endless!

Loaded Veggie Dawgs

Serves: 6   Skill Level: **Easy**   Prep Time: **25 to 30 minutes**   Cook Time: **5 minutes**

You can make these the light way and use veggie dogs, or you can be a little more decadent and use a regular hot dog. Either way, these loaded veggie *dawgs* aren't like anything you've ever had. That is unless you're familiar with Vietnamese *báhn mì* sandwiches, 'cause that's the inspiration at work here. *Báhn mì* are explosions of different textures and flavors and are surprisingly easy to mimic using hot dogs and hot dog buns. If you like crunchy, sweet, salty, and sour all in one mouthwatering bite, get to work making these puppies.

FOR THE DOGS:

6 hot dogs, butterflied lengthwise

6 whole-wheat hot dog buns, toasted and scooped out

FOR THE TOPPINGS:

Pickled carrots and daikon, recipe follows

½ English cucumber, cut in half lengthwise and thinly sliced

½ bunch fresh mint

1 jalapeño, thinly sliced, optional

Sliced scallions, to serve

FOR THE PICKLED CARROTS AND DAIKON:

2 carrots, peeled and grated

1 daikon radish, peeled and grated, or 1 bunch red radish

1 teaspoon kosher salt

1 teaspoon granulated sugar

2 tablespoons white vinegar

FOR THE SPICY MAYO:

1 cup mayonnaise

1–2 tablespoons sriracha hot sauce

Pinch of salt

TO MAKE THE DOGS:

1. Heat a griddle over medium-high heat. Make sure the griddle is oiled lightly.

2. Place the hot dogs cut-side down on the griddle and cook for 1 minute, just until crispy. Flip and cook on the skin side for 1 more minute.

3. Remove and place on the bun, cut-side up. Serve with your choice of toppings and spicy mayo.

TO MAKE THE PICKLED CARROTS AND DAIKON:

4. Combine the ingredients in a bowl and toss to coat.

5. Transfer to a colander and place over a bowl. Allow to sit for 5 to 10 minutes to pickle.

6. Squeeze out the excess liquid; discard. Set pickles aside until ready to use. The pickles can be made a few days in advance and stored in the fridge for up to a week.

TO MAKE THE SPICY MAYO:

7. Stir together the ingredients until combined. Adjust hot sauce to taste.

MICHAEL
Pickling your own veggies is easy. All you need is vinegar, salt, and sugar. Feel free to play with different spices and flavor combinations.

Bloody Mary Sliders

Serves: **Makes 12 sliders**   Skill Level: **Easy**   Prep Time: **30 minutes**   Cook Time: **4 to 6 minutes**

These burgers are inspired by my favorite Sunday morning (and afternoon) drink. Who doesn't love a Sunday brunch with a Bloody Mary? But I also love burgers, and in a "chocolate plus peanut butter is twice the yum" kind of move, I decided that these two great things belong together. Think about what goes in a Bloody Mary (tomato juice, Worcestershire sauce, horseradish . . .); these ingredients are reminiscent of a lot of condiments we normally put on *top* of our burgers. I just up the ante on my sliders, getting all those great flavors right in the mix!

2 ¼ pounds ground beef (80 percent lean)

3 tablespoons Worcestershire sauce

1 tablespoon ground celery seeds

1 tablespoon freshly ground black pepper

Kosher salt, to taste

1 cup grated sharp cheddar cheese

½ cup cream cheese, softened

1 tablespoon Dijon mustard

1 tablespoon prepared horseradish

Extra-virgin olive oil, for grilling

½ cup ketchup

1 teaspoon hot sauce

Potato slider rolls, to serve

Olives, to serve

Mayonnaise, to serve

Pickles, to serve

1. In a large bowl, mix together the beef, Worcestershire sauce, ground celery seeds, pepper, and salt, but do not overwork. In a medium bowl, combine the two cheeses, mustard, and horseradish. Portion the meat into 12, 3-ounce balls. Press flat and place a heaping tablespoon of the cheese mixture in the center. Bring up the edges of the meat to completely cover the cheese and flatten slightly to form a thick stuffed patty. Repeat with the remaining meat and filling.

2. Heat a griddle or nonstick pan over medium-high heat. Drizzle the patties with olive oil and place them on the grill. Cook for 2 to 3 minutes on the first side and flip to cook for 2 to 3 more minutes on the second side. Remove from the grill and serve on a potato slider roll. Skewer with a toothpick and olive.

3. Serve with an assortment of condiments. To make spicy ketchup, combine ½ cup ketchup with 1 teaspoon hot sauce.

MARIO
I think a griddle is the best way to cook a hamburger. I love the effect of a charcoal grill, but a griddle gives it that crispy crust.

Corn Apple Salad

Serves: 4   Skill Level: **Easy**   Prep Time: **10 minutes**   Cook Time: **6 to 8 minutes**

I'm all about the sides that are served at a barbecue. Obviously, corn has to be on the table! Instead of opting for plain old corn on the cob, I do a corn salad that's smoky, sweet, crunchy, and has a tiny bit of heat. If you're serving it with barbecued meat, the fresh flavors will perfectly offset the richness of the meat and the tiny bit of smokiness will tie it all together. And it doesn't hurt that this salad helps to make your table look beautiful!

4 ears of corn, husks and silk removed

⅓ cup, plus 2 tablespoons extra-virgin olive oil

1 apple, cored and finely diced to the size of corn kernels

¼ cup fresh chives, chopped

2 tablespoons fresh tarragon, chopped

1 shallot, finely diced

3 tablespoons apple cider vinegar

1 tablespoon Dijon mustard

Salt

Freshly ground black pepper

1. Preheat a gas or stovetop grill to medium-high.

2. Drizzle the corn with 2 tablespoons olive oil and place on the grill, turning occasionally, until lightly charred on all sides, 6 to 8 minutes. Remove from the grill and cut kernels from the cob.

3. Whisk together the apple, chives, tarragon, shallot, vinegar, mustard, salt, and pepper. Add remaining ⅓ cup of olive oil in a steady stream while whisking to create vinaigrette. Adjust seasoning to taste. Toss in the corn to coat.

4. Serve warm or at room temperature.

PAGES 36-37: Chef Ming Tsai joins the hosts as they cook up their favorite patriotic plates.

Potato Salad

Serves: 6 to 8   Skill Level: Easy   Prep Time: 15 minutes   Cook Time: 15 to 20 minutes

Bacon shouldn't be an everyday indulgence, but for special occasions, it definitely ups the delicious factor of any dish. This potato salad combines the smoky lushness of bacon with the cool creaminess of the side dish we all know and love. But then it really sings with a spicy kick from the combo of mustard and scallions, and tanginess from red wine vinegar. When you put this on the table, the potato salad connoisseurs in your crowd will bow down. You can't do better than this.

2 ½ pounds baby Yukon Gold potatoes, skin on

¼ pound bacon, cooked and crumbled

½ cup mayonnaise

2 tablespoons whole-grain mustard

2 tablespoons red wine vinegar

1 teaspoon sugar

4 scallions, sliced on a bias

Salt and pepper, to taste

1. Place potatoes in a pot, cover with cold water, season with a generous pinch of salt, and bring to a boil. Cook potatoes until fork-tender, 15 to 20 minutes.

2. Drain potatoes and slice in half.

3. In a large bowl, whisk together the bacon, mayonnaise, mustard, vinegar, sugar, scallions, and a pinch of salt and pepper. Add the potatoes to the dressing and toss everything to coat. Adjust seasoning to taste before serving.

Grilled Banana Boat

Serves: 2   Skill Level: **Easy**   Prep Time: **20 minutes**   Cook Time: **10 to 15 minutes**

Summertime means different things for different folks, but everyone seems to have fond memories of campfires. Campfires usually conjure up thoughts of hot dogs, potatoes in aluminum foil, and, of course, s'mores. This recipe is a new one to add to your outdoor repertoire. It's basically a new twist on a banana split; with warm grilled fruit and cold ice cream giving the perfect contrast . . . who wouldn't love it?

½ pound cherries, pitted, plus two cherries for garnish

3 tablespoons sugar

Juice and zest of 1 lemon

1 tablespoon cornstarch

1 banana, split in half lengthwise, peel on

Vegetable oil, for grilling

Vanilla ice cream, to serve

Chocolate sauce, to serve

Whipped cream, to serve

Crushed peanuts, to serve

1. Preheat a gas or stovetop grill to medium-high.

2. In a medium bowl, combine the pitted cherries, sugar, lemon juice and zest, and cornstarch. Transfer mixture to a large piece of aluminum foil and fold up to form a packet. Grill the packet on a low-heat section of the grill until the cherries have broken down and formed a sauce, 10 to 15 minutes.

3. Brush the banana halves with vegetable oil and place, skin-side down, on the grill for 2 minutes.

4. Remove to plate. Top banana halves with ice cream, chocolate sauce, whipped cream, nuts, a drizzle of the cherry sauce, and remaining 2 cherries.

Key Lime Pie Pops

Serves: 8   **Skill Level: Easy**   **Prep Time: 20 minutes**   **Inactive Prep Time: 2 hours**

I first discovered key lime pie when I was on the beach in Florida. It's so delicious but, let's face it, not the healthiest thing on earth. When I'm in the mood for key lime pie, I whip out this family-friendly recipe. The whole shebang comes in at an economical buck a pop and is under 140 calories per serving. And if you're feeling innovative, you can use it at a dinner party as a palate cleanser instead of the usual sorbet. So refreshing!

3 tablespoons honey

3 cups plain Greek yogurt

Zest of 3 key limes, divided

⅓ cup key lime juice

1 tablespoon vanilla extract

1 cup crushed graham crackers, divided

SPECIAL EQUIPMENT:

8, 3-ounce paper cups

8 ice-pop sticks

1. Combine the honey, yogurt, zest of 2 limes, lime juice, vanilla extract, and ½ cup of crushed graham crackers in the bowl of an electric mixer.

2. Beat at medium-high speed until smooth and creamy.

3. In a small bowl, combine the zest of 1 lime and ½ cup crushed graham crackers, and divide evenly among 8 paper cups.

4. Divide yogurt mixture equally among cups, so that each is about three-quarters full. Insert ice-pop sticks.

5. Freeze for at least 2 hours, until set. Remove from the freezer and remove the paper cups. Serve immediately.

DAPHNE
The portion size of these pops is perfect for kids, and they're a healthy alternative to other sugary treats.

Dip-Dye Napkins

When we think of tie-dye, we think of old clothes from the sixties and a few fashion mistakes that have popped up since then. But dip-dyeing is a newer, fresher way to get your napkins (or any other fabric you may want to work with) to become the life of the party. Poor old tie-dye, it's become the poster child for fashion failure. Dip-dyeing is your new way to create a table that broadcasts just how fashion-forward you really are.

White cloth napkins or table runner (should be at least 50 percent cotton)

Liquid fabric dye

A heatproof container, approximately the height of your folded fabric

A yardstick or wooden dowel

Salt, about 1 cup

Rubber gloves

1. Fill the container about one-third or halfway with hot water, depending on how high you want the dye to go.

2. Add the fabric dye to the water. Follow the package instructions, but for lighter colors, use less dye. Remember, the material will dry lighter than it appears when wet.

3. Stir the salt into the hot water. The salt helps the dye adhere to the fabric.

4. Dampen your fabric under the tap, then drape over the yardstick.

5. Balance the yardstick on the edges of the container so the bottom of the fabric is submerged in liquid.

6. Allow the fabric to soak in the dye until you have achieved your desired results. The longer it soaks, the darker the color will be. For an ombré effect, gradually add water every few minutes to dilute the dye and raise the water level.

Shown at right with the Dip-Dye Napkin is Daphne's Corn Apple Salad. For the recipe, turn to page 38.

LABOR DAY PICNIC

Sparkling Basil Lemonade

Serves: **6**   Skill Level: **Easy**   Prep Time: **10 minutes**   Cook Time: **10 to 15 minutes**

This sparkling lemonade is doubly refreshing: it's got the thirst-quenching qualities of lemons and the herbal freshness of basil. Add the kick of vodka to the mix and you've got the ultimate summertime cocktail. If you're feeling like a teetotaler, leave out the liquor and pour over ice. Now kick back, relax, and sip away.

FOR THE BASIL SIMPLE SYRUP:

1 cup water

1 cup sugar

¼ cup packed basil leaves

FOR THE SPARKLING LEMONADE:

4 cups freshly squeezed lemon juice

8 ounces vodka

6 ounces basil simple syrup

Soda water, to finish

TO MAKE THE BASIL SIMPLE SYRUP:

1. Bring water and sugar to a boil and stir until sugar has dissolved, about 8 minutes. Remove from heat and add basil leaves. Allow to steep until syrup is room temperature. Remove basil leaves and chill syrup in the fridge until ready to use.

TO MAKE THE SPARKLING LEMONADE:

2. Stir together the lemon juice, vodka, and simple syrup. Serve over ice and top off with soda water.

DAPHNE
I use mason jars all summer long. I love them. They are good for hot and cold drinks.

CLINTON
Mason jars are awesome. They automatically give you that picnic feel.

Giant Italian Hero

Serves: 6 **Skill Level: Easy** **Prep Time: 45 minutes** Cook Time: **15 to 20 minutes**
Inactive Cook Time: **24 hours**

Scarlett O'Hara and Rhett Butler. Elizabeth Bennet and Mr. Darcy. Lucy and Ricky Ricardo. Each person is a powerhouse unto himself or herself, but when you put them together, these couples are dynamite. It's exactly the same with the Giant Italian Hero. Eggplant parmigiana and the Italian sub are classics in their own right. But combine them into one recipe and presto! It's a sandwich match made in heaven.

FOR SPICY CELERY GIARDINIERA:

1 pound celery, sliced thin

2 jalapeños, seeded, stems removed, sliced into thin rings

1 Fresno chili, seeded, stem removed, sliced into thin rings

2 cloves garlic, minced

1 small red onion, sliced thin

1 teaspoon ancho chili powder

1 teaspoon salt

1 teaspoon freshly ground black pepper

1 tablespoon toasted coriander seeds

1/4 cup flat-leaf parsley, chopped

4 ounces red wine vinegar

4 ounces extra-virgin olive oil

FOR GIANT ITALIAN HERO:

1 1/2 cups flour

3 eggs, lightly beaten

1 1/2 cups bread crumbs

Salt and freshly ground black pepper, to taste

TO MAKE SPICY CELERY GIARDINIERA:

1. Combine all ingredients, mix well, and marinate for 24 hours in the refrigerator. This can keep for up to two weeks.

TO MAKE GIANT ITALIAN HERO:

2. Place the flour, eggs, and bread crumbs in three separate dishes for dredging. Season each with salt and pepper. Lightly coat the pieces of eggplant in flour, coat in egg, and cover completely in the bread crumbs.

3. Heat olive oil in a large nonstick skillet over medium-high heat.

4. Fry the dredged pieces of eggplant on both sides until golden, about 3 minutes per side. Remove to a paper towel–lined plate and season immediately with salt.

5. Begin to assemble the sandwich starting with the basil leaves. Place torn basil leaves on one side of the bread. Top with layers of sliced meats. Place fried eggplant down and top with fresh mozzarella and spicy celery giardiniera.

6. Close the sandwich and enjoy.

2 medium eggplants, peeled and sliced into ½-inch-thick pieces

3 tablespoons olive oil

6 hoagie rolls, split lengthwise and pressed open

1 bunch fresh basil

1 pound sliced mortadella

1 pound sliced salami

1 pound sliced *soppressata*

2 pounds sliced fresh mozzarella

Sweet Potato Chips

Serves: **4**   Skill Level: **Easy**   Prep Time: **10 minutes**   Cook Time: **1 to 1½ hours**

It's no secret that baking potato chips is a healthier way to prepare a crunchy snack. But these baked chips do have a little secret. Cinnamon and salt are the unlikely combination that makes these sweet potato chips even sweeter and more savory than the usual variety. These are a perfect pairing for sandwiches, salads, or soups.

2 large sweet potatoes

1–2 teaspoons cinnamon

2 tablespoons olive oil

Salt, to taste

DAPHNE
Wait until you hear the calorie difference. For a cup of these chips, it's less than 100 calories. For a cup of potato chips, it's 200 calories.

1. Preheat oven to 250°F.

2. Scrub the potatoes under running water until clean.

3. Using a mandoline or a knife, slice the potatoes lengthwise into thin slices, about ⅛-inch thick.

4. In a large bowl, toss sliced potatoes with olive oil and sprinkle with cinnamon and salt.

5. Lay out on parchment-lined sheet trays and cook for 1 to 1½ hours, flipping halfway through the cooking process.

6. Remove from the oven once crisp and slightly golden brown. Season with additional salt if desired.

Three-Bean Salad

Serves: **6**   Skill Level: **Easy**   Prep Time: **30 minutes**   Cook Time: **10 minutes**

Is it even possible to have a picnic without a three-bean salad? Of course not! Three-bean salads are a perennial favorite for a lot of good reasons: they travel well, the beans soak up the dressing and become even more scrumptious the longer they marinate, they're full of protein and good for you . . . the list goes on. This particular salad brings a little bit of the south of France to your table by adding a pistou to the dressing. The flavors are fresh, bright, and gorgeously fragrant. What more could you ask for?

FOR THE PISTOU:

1 bunch parsley

½ cup extra-virgin olive oil

1 garlic clove, finely minced

Salt and freshly ground pepper, to taste

Zest of 1 lemon

FOR THE SALAD:

2 tablespoons olive oil

1 red onion, small dice

2 ribs celery, small dice, divided

Salt, to taste

2 garlic cloves, minced

1, 14-ounce can small red kidney beans, drained and rinsed

1, 14-ounce can black beans, drained and rinsed

1, 14-ounce can cannellini beans, drained and rinsed

Freshly ground black pepper, to taste

¼ cup pistou

Chili oil, to finish

TO MAKE THE PISTOU:

1. Combine the ingredients in a food processor and pulse until slightly chunky. Season with salt and pepper to taste.

TO MAKE THE SALAD:

2. In a large sauté pan, heat olive oil. Add the onion and half of the celery and season with salt. Sauté until just soft, about 3 minutes.

3. Add the garlic and remaining celery, cooking until fragrant. Stir in beans to warm through.

4. Remove from heat and transfer to a bowl. Add the pistou and toss everything to coat. Season to taste with salt and freshly ground pepper. Finish with the chili oil.

Blueberry Pucker Bars

Serves: 9   Skill Level: **Moderate**   Prep Time: **40 minutes**   Cook Time: **35 to 40 minutes**

What goes together just as well as strawberries and cream, if not better? Blueberries and lemon! When blueberries are in season (which is the case around Labor Day so you *better* make these bars for your late-summer picnic), there is no excuse not to make these! You can't help but pucker up with all the different ways that lemon shows up in these bars . . . so gobble them up and send summer off with a kiss.

FOR THE BLUEBERRY PUCKER BARS:

2 cups self-rising flour

1 cup granulated sugar, divided

Pinch of salt

Zest and juice of 1 lemon

1 large egg yolk whisked with 1 tablespoon water

10 tablespoons cold butter, cubed, plus more for greasing the pan

1 tablespoon cornstarch

3 cups blueberries, fresh or frozen

FOR THE LEMON CREAM:

½ cup heavy cream

1 tablespoon granulated sugar

¼ cup lemon curd

TO MAKE THE BLUEBERRY PUCKER BARS:

1. Preheat oven to 350°F. Grease a 9- x 9-inch baking dish with butter.

2. Whisk together the flour, ⅔ cup sugar, salt, and lemon zest in a large bowl. Stir in the egg yolk mixture. Working with your hands, blend in the cubed butter.

3. Press all but 1½ cups of the mixture into the bottom of the prepared baking dish.

4. In a medium bowl, toss together the blueberries, lemon juice, remaining sugar, and cornstarch. Pour mixture over the crust. Crumble the remaining flour mixture over the blueberries.

5. Bake for 35 to 40 minutes or until topping is golden and blueberries are cooked down.

6. Remove from oven and allow to cool to room temperature before serving with a dollop of lemon cream.

TO MAKE THE LEMON CREAM:

7. With an electric mixer, whip heavy cream and sugar on high speed to medium-stiff peaks. Fold in the curd and serve.

Daphne's Darn Those Bugs

Let's get real: bugs might be cute when they pop up in cartoons and movies, but when they pop up on *you* they're much less adorable. Here's a fabulous nontoxic way to keep the bugs at bay while you're out having a good time. And the best part of my all-natural bug spray? It makes you smell great, not like a chemistry lab. Bugs begone!

1 cup distilled water

1 stem fresh citronella

3 tablespoons dried lavender

1 tablespoon whole cloves

4 tablespoons dried peppermint

1 cup rubbing alcohol

1. Bring the distilled water to a boil in a small saucepan. As soon as it's simmering, crush the citronella in your fingers and add it, along with the lavender, cloves, and mint, to the water.

2. Remove from heat and cover. Allow to cool completely.

3. Add the rubbing alcohol. Pour the mixture through a strainer lined with a coffee filter into a spray bottle.

4. Store in a cool place for up to three months.

MICHAEL
Here's a fun fact for all you entomologists out there: the smell of plants in the mint family is actually repulsive to bugs. We love it, but bugs hate it!

HAPPY HOLIDAYS!

It's impossible to hear the word *holiday* without thinking of food. What is Thanksgiving without a turkey? Christmas without cookies? Easter without chocolate eggs? Hanukkah without latkes? Halloween without candy corn? Okay, you get the point. Every family has different traditions and menus for their holiday celebrations, but the universal ingredients are good food and people you love.

At *The Chew* we have our own tight-knit family, and consequently, our own recipes for merrymaking. And now, in the spirit of giving, we are going to share those recipes with you. What follows are our suggestions for how to make the most of our favorite holidays by creating excellent food, ambience, and memories.

HALLOWEEN

Psychorita

Serves: **1**   Skill Level: **Easy**   Prep Time: **5 minutes**

What's one of the best movies to watch during Halloween? *Psycho*! And what's the tastiest twist on a margarita? A Psychorita! Whether or not you know a psycho named Rita is immaterial to enjoying this cocktail. You can mix up this juicy drink just before curling up for a monster-movie marathon, or make a big batch for a ghoulish gathering. But be wary: it's so good, it's scary.

1 lime wedge

Red finishing sugar

1 ounce lime juice

1 tablespoon agave syrup

2 ounces pomegranate juice

2 ounces silver tequila

½ ounce orange liqueur

1 ounce orange juice

Pomegranate seeds, for garnish, optional

1. Rub the rim of a margarita glass with a lime wedge, then invert onto a plate of red finishing sugar to coat.

2. Pour remaining ingredients into a cocktail shaker filled with ice and shake vigorously until cold. Pour into a glass and garnish with pomegranate seeds, if desired.

CLINTON
Before every party, I obsessively make lists and timelines and check them ten times, so I don't forget anything. But I always make it look like I'm stress-free! That's the key to a great shindig—a relaxed host.

Chicken Diablo

Serves: **4 to 6**   Skill Level: **Easy**   Prep Time: **5 minutes**   Cook Time: **10 to 15 minutes**

The devil is in the details with this diabolically delectable dish. If you leave out the jalapeño pepper, you've got a tasty dinner that may or may not live on in your family's collective memory. Throw that jalapeño in there and you've got *Diablo!* It's spicy, extra flavorful, and (admit it) fun to say. If you're having a Halloween party and are looking for the right meal to serve before you hit the streets looking for candy, this is the one. Whether you wear your angel or devil costume is entirely up to you.

¼ cup olive oil

6, 4-ounce boneless skin-on chicken thighs, pounded to a ¼-inch thickness

Kosher salt and freshly ground black pepper

2 garlic cloves, sliced

1 red bell pepper, stem and seeds removed, thinly sliced

1 jalapeño, stem and seeds removed, sliced into rings, optional

1, 14-ounce can crushed San Marzano tomatoes

2 tablespoons capers, rinsed and drained

½ cup fresh flat-leaf parsley leaves, roughly chopped

1. Place a Dutch oven or deep cast-iron skillet over medium-high heat. Add the olive oil to the preheated pan. Season both sides of the chicken with salt and pepper. Put the chicken skin-side down in the pan and cook until golden brown, 2 to 3 minutes. Flip the chicken and cook for another 2 minutes. Add the garlic, bell pepper, jalapeño, and a pinch of salt, and cook for another 2 to 3 minutes.

2. Add ½ cup water, scraping with a wooden spoon to incorporate the browned bits on the bottom of the pan. Cook until the liquid is reduced by half, another 3 minutes. Add the tomatoes and capers, cover the pan, and cook for 5 more minutes.

3. Remove the pan from the heat and stir in the parsley. Taste and adjust the seasoning, adding salt and pepper as needed. Serve immediately.

Trick or Treat Mac and Cheese

Serves: 8 to 10   Skill Level: **Easy**   Prep Time: **20 minutes**   Cook Time: **15 to 20 minutes**

Fall, and consequently Halloween, brings with it a host of veggies that are just plain good. They're good for you, they taste good, and they look good. But what if you're not a veggie person? What do you do with all that fall has to offer in the way of squash (like butternut or even pumpkin), kale, and all those excellent root vegetables? That's an easy one. Add cheese, bacon, and pasta: the holy trinity of awesome. What you wind up with is Trick or Treat Mac and Cheese; it may seem like a trick, but take one bite and you can't deny it's a treat.

2 tablespoons salt

1 pound rigatoni

1 pound bacon, diced

3 tablespoons butter

1 onion, diced

1 butternut squash, peeled and diced

2 cups black kale, de-ribbed and chopped

2 cloves garlic, minced

3 tablespoons flour

3 cups milk

⅓ cup half-and-half

1 cup unsweetened pumpkin puree

1½ cups Gruyère cheese

1 teaspoon nutmeg, freshly grated

½ cup mascarpone

1–2 tablespoons chipotle powder, optional

Kosher salt and freshly ground black pepper, to taste

2 cups bread crumbs

¼ cup parsley, chopped

1. Bring 6 quarts of water to a boil in a large pot. Add salt and pasta. Cook the rigatoni in boiling water 3 minutes less than the package instructs. Drain, then set aside.

2. In a Dutch oven, over medium heat, cook the bacon until crisp. Add the butter and onions and cook until translucent. Add the butternut squash, kale, and garlic and cook about 6 more minutes until kale has wilted. Add the flour and stir to make a roux. Cook for 2 more minutes, stirring constantly. Slowly pour in the milk and half-and-half and bring the mixture to simmer. Stir in the pumpkin puree. Cook gently until the mixture thickens, 4 to 5 minutes. Add 1 cup of the Gruyère and the nutmeg, and stir until all of the cheese is melted. Add the mascarpone and mix until melted and combined. Stir in the chipotle and add the cooked rigatoni. Toss pasta until it is well mixed. Season with salt and pepper to taste.

3. Situate top rack in oven so that once Dutch oven is placed inside, the top will be about six inches from the heating source. Preheat the oven to broil. Sprinkle the bread crumbs over the casserole. Broil for about 1 minute, or until the topping is crunchy and golden.

4. Garnish with parsley and serve hot.

Caramel Apples

Serves: **6**   Skill Level: **Moderate**   Prep Time: **15 minutes**   Cook Time: **25 to 30 minutes**
Inactive Cook Time: **10 minutes**

Salted caramel has swept the nation. You can find it in ice cream, candies, cupcake frosting—the list goes on. But now we have put that perfect combo to good use in yet another way. We've taken the Halloween and fairground treat and, with a few additions, brought caramel apples up to date. Give them a try, particularly using dainty lady apples; they're so petite you don't have to worry if you eat more than one!

6 Granny Smith, honey crisp, or Pink Lady apples

1 cup honey

1 cup heavy cream

1/2 teaspoon salt

1/2 cup peanuts, chopped

1/2 cup almonds, chopped

1/2 cup walnuts, chopped

1 tablespoon flaky sea salt

SPECIAL EQUIPMENT:

6 craft sticks

Candy thermometer

1. Bring a small pot of water to a rolling boil. Dip each apple in the boiling water, then wipe dry with a paper towel to remove wax coating. Set aside. Remove the stem of each apple, and insert a craft stick in its place.

2. In a medium, heavy-bottomed pot over medium-high heat, combine the honey, cream, and salt. Bring mixture to a boil, and then reduce heat until it simmers. Using a candy thermometer to read the temperature, bring to a reading of 265°F, stirring slowly and often, 20 to 25 minutes. Remove from heat.

3. Place a sheet of parchment or wax paper on a baking sheet, and coat lightly with nonstick spray. Carefully twirl each apple in the caramel mixture and set on prepared sheet. On individual plates, place the peanuts, almonds, walnuts, and sea salt. After caramel has cooled slightly, about 10 minutes, fold the pooled coating on the bottom of the apple upward. Roll in desired toppings, and serve.

CARLA
I'm constantly stimulated by all the ideas from the other hosts. I find that I want to entertain more so I can share what I learn: a place setting, a new twist on a dish, a new technique. The discovery is fun and exciting.

Candy Surprise Cupcakes

Serves: 12   Skill Level: Moderate   Prep Time: 25 to 30 minutes   Cook Time: 12 to 14 minutes

Halloween may be known for the spooky stuff: haunted houses, goblins, and ghouls. But any kid worth his or her salt knows that the most exciting part is the trick-or-treating. Trick-or-treating is so much fun because not only do you get candy, but also the type of candy you get at each house or apartment is a surprise. These tricky treats are like trick-or-treating in baked form; you know you're going to bite into a delicious candy-topped cupcake, but you don't realize there's more candy inside until . . . surprise!

FOR THE CUPCAKES:

6 ounces unsalted butter, room temperature

¾ cup granulated sugar

½ cup light brown sugar

3 eggs, room temperature

2 cups all-purpose flour

2 teaspoons baking powder

Pinch of salt

¾ cup milk

½ teaspoon vanilla extract

Chocolate-flavored mini Halloween candy bars

FOR THE FROSTING:

1 pound whipped cream cheese, room temperature

4 ounces unsalted butter, room temperature

2 cups confectioners' sugar

SPECIAL EQUIPMENT:

Muffin liners

12-count muffin tin

TO MAKE THE CUPCAKES:

1. Preheat oven to 350°F. Line muffin tin with cupcake liners. In a large bowl, beat together the butter and sugars with an electric mixer until light and fluffy, about 5 minutes. Whip in the eggs until fully combined.

2. In a medium bowl, whisk together the flour, baking powder, and salt. In a small bowl, combine the milk and the vanilla extract. Add one third of the dry mixture to the sugar mix and blend, then add half of the milk. Alternate with the remaining flour and milk, ending with the flour.

3. Evenly divide the batter among the cupcake liners. Press one 1-inch piece of candy in the center of each cupcake (taking note of the order of the candy for later). Bake for 12 to 14 minutes or until light gold on top. Remove from oven and allow to cool on a wire rack. Decorate with frosting and garnish with additional pieces of candy that match the candy inside.

TO MAKE THE FROSTING:

4. Beat together the cream cheese and butter until fluffy, about 5 minutes. Add the sugar and beat in until fully incorporated. This can be made a few days in advance and kept covered in the fridge. Return to room temperature when ready to use.

Psyllium Slime

Here's a riddle: how can you freak out your kids, give them something cool and gross to play with, and pay pennies for it? Make psyllium slime! Using psyllium husks (or powdered fiber supplement if you have it on hand) and a few other ingredients that are supercheap, you can make slime for a haunted house, whip up a nontoxic toy for your kids to get messy with, or even decorate your front door with when trick-or-treaters come knocking. That's right, you can be the slimiest family on the block using not much more than water and your trusty fiber supplement! What are you waiting for?

1 teaspoon psyllium husks (or powdered fiber supplement)

1 cup water

Food coloring

1. Whisk the psyllium into the water and add your favorite food coloring.

2. Place the bowl in the microwave and cook on high for 4 to 5 minutes (actual time depends on microwave power) or until the goo is about to bubble over the sides of the bowl.

3. Let the mixture cool slightly, then repeat preceding step 4 to 5 more times. The more times this step is repeated, the more rubbery the substance will become. Let it cool and then play!

DAPHNE
When I was in kindergarten, I was obsessed with Ariel from *The Little Mermaid*. So my mother and I dyed my hair red that year, we sewed a little purple felt brassiere to a leotard suit, and put on a green skirt for the tail. I remember that costume so well.

The cast of *The Middle* (Charlie McDermott, Atticus Shaffer, Eden Sher, Patricia Heaton, and Neil Flynn) join *The Chew* cohosts in a spook-tacular Halloween celebration.

THANKSGIVING

Cider Sangria

Serves: **4 to 6**   Skill Level: **Easy**   Prep Time: **15 minutes**

The apple is a majestic fruit. Take a moment to reflect . . . apples are pretty enough to be used as centerpieces, they taste great right off the tree, they make the best baked goods, *and* they can be made into great booze. Hard apple cider and apple brandy (also known as Calvados) are truly in the category of Nectar of the Gods. With that in mind, if you mix your cider and brandy with a few other key ingredients, it's a pretty safe bet you're going to come up with something out of this world!

2 green or red apples, cored, quartered, and thinly sliced

1 navel orange, quartered and thinly sliced crosswise

1 cup apple juice, chilled

2 tablespoons fresh lemon juice

¼ cup apple brandy

1, 22-ounce bottle hard apple cider, chilled

Ice

1. In a pitcher, combine the apples with the orange, apple juice, lemon juice, and brandy.

2. Before serving, add the hard cider. Serve in tall glasses with ice.

MARIO
Thanks to Clinton, I'm making better, tastier, and more interesting cocktails. Easiest way to liven up a party!

Crispy Shallot Green Bean Casserole

Serves: 6 to 8   Skill Level: **Easy**   Prep Time: **20 minutes**   Cook Time: **25 to 30 minutes**

It's always fun to take a classic and make it your own. Green bean casserole is one of those tried-and-true favorites that show up at Thanksgiving, Christmas, potlucks, you name it. But I think it's time for good ol' green bean casserole to get a new lease on life. Instead of using canned fried onions, I've got homemade crispy shallots, which are much more flavorful than the ready-made onions we know so well. And my green beans even get a little spa treatment of their own—they soak in a bath of seasoned water that plumps them up and makes them worthy of their shallot-y friends. Watch your guests' faces when they take a bite of this beauty; they'll be expecting the usual but will get the WOW!

3 cups vegetable oil

Salt, to taste

4 shallots, 1 chopped and 3 thinly sliced, divided

1½ cups buttermilk

1 cup, plus 2 tablespoons flour, divided

½ teaspoon cayenne pepper

1½ pounds green beans, ends trimmed

3 tablespoons butter

2 garlic cloves, thinly sliced

1 cup chicken stock

1 cup half-and-half

Freshly ground black pepper, to taste

2 cups freshly grated Parmesan

1. Preheat oven to 375°F. Heat the vegetable oil in a large, high-sided cast-iron skillet. Bring a large pot of water to a boil and season liberally with salt. Place the thinly sliced shallots in a medium bowl and pour the buttermilk over them. Toss the shallots to separate the pieces and completely coat.

2. In another bowl or shallow dish, whisk together 1 cup of flour and the cayenne just until combined. Remove some shallots from the buttermilk and dredge in the seasoned flour mixture. Shake off any excess flour and gently place in the heated oil. Fry until golden and crispy, about 1 minute. Using a heatproof slotted spoon, remove the shallots to a paper towel–lined plate. Fry the remaining sliced shallots in batches. Season with salt to taste.

3. Prepare a large bowl with water and ice along with a strainer. Cook the green beans in the boiling water for 1 minute; then remove and immediately plunge into the ice bath. Allow beans to cool completely, then remove to a paper towel–lined plate to dry.

4. While the beans are cooling and drying, melt the butter in a sauté pan over medium heat. Add the chopped shallot and season with salt. Cook until soft, about 3 minutes, then add garlic and cook just until fragrant, another minute. Sprinkle remaining 2 tablespoons of flour into the pan and stir to coat shallots and garlic. Slowly whisk in the

CARLA
Every season I look forward to Thanksgiving on the show, because all of the other hosts have fun sides and holiday dishes that I drool over.

chicken stock, whisking out any lumps. Whisk in the half-and-half and season to taste with salt and pepper. Simmer for 2 minutes or just until thickened. Stir in the cheese and remove from heat.

5. Combine the beans and onion sauce in a 9- x 9-inch casserole dish and bake for 20 to 25 minutes. The liquid should reduce and thicken. Remove from the oven and top with crispy shallots. Cool slightly before serving.

Turkey Gravy

Serves: **Makes 1 quart**   Skill Level: **Easy**   Prep Time: **20 minutes**   Cook Time: **1 hour**

French fries and ketchup, ice cream and hot fudge, turkey and gravy. Some foods just aren't the same without the topping that goes with them. You can't have a great Thanksgiving bird without rich gravy to enhance the flavor and mingle a little with all the other good stuff hanging out on your plate. This recipe is the original, the godmother of all turkey gravies, if you will. Easy, low cost, and foolproof, it's a winner; just make sure you make enough!

2 tablespoons olive oil

1 turkey neck

4 tablespoons unsalted butter

1 cup onion, medium dice

½ cup celery, medium dice

½ cup carrots, medium dice

1 small bunch fresh thyme

1 bay leaf

Pinch of salt

4 tablespoons flour

4 cups turkey or chicken stock

Drippings from roast turkey

1. Place stockpot over medium-high heat. When the pan is hot, add the olive oil along with the turkey neck. Brown the neck on all sides, about 5 minutes. Remove to a plate, and then add the butter to the pan.

2. When the butter has melted, add the onion, celery, carrot, thyme, bay leaf, and salt. Cook, stirring occasionally, for about 10 minutes, until all of the vegetables are aromatic and slightly caramelized.

3. Next stir in the flour to coat the vegetables and absorb the butter. Add the turkey neck back to the pan. Whisk in the stock and bring to a gentle boil. Reduce the heat to medium and simmer, stirring occasionally for 45 minutes.

4. After 45 minutes, whisk in any pan drippings from roasting your turkey, and give the gravy a taste, adding more seasoning if necessary. Strain, discarding solids, and keep warm.

MICHAEL
Everything I do on *The Chew* is a reflection of how Liz and I entertain at home. My goal is always to show people how we do it at our own house because we always have so much fun.

Turkey with Grapefruit and Tapenade

Serves: **8 to 10**   Skill Level: **Moderate**   Prep Time: **20 minutes**   Cook Time: **3 ½ to 4 hours**
Inactive Cook Time: **12 hours**

The secret to a tender bird is a step that many Thanksgiving hosts overlook: brining. You've gotta brine your bird if you want the meat to be flavorful and moist. There are a few different takes on which brine is the best, so I've shared the one I think is the hands-down winner. But if you want to infuse even more flavor into a turkey or any bird you're roasting, spreading tasty concoctions between the meat and the skin does the trick. I've gone with a Mediterranean option: rich olive tapenade, which is offset by the bright citrus of the grapefruit making a cameo appearance in the turkey while it roasts. *Perfezione!*

1 gallon water

1 cup salt

2 cups honey

1 gallon ice water

1, 12- to 15-pound turkey

½ cup black olive tapenade

¼ cup olive oil

Zest of 2 oranges

1 onion, chopped

1 bunch scallions

1 grapefruit, peeled and chopped

1. In a large stockpot over high heat, combine the water, salt, and honey. Bring to a boil, and stir frequently to be sure salt is dissolved. Remove from heat, and let cool to room temperature. When the mixture is cool, pour it into a clean 5-gallon bucket. Stir in the ice water.

2. Place the turkey, "head first," into the brine. Make sure that the cavity gets filled. Place the bucket in the refrigerator overnight, but no longer than 12 hours. Remove the turkey and carefully drain off the excess brine and pat dry. Discard the excess brine. Preheat the oven to 425°F. Place an oven rack in the lower third of the oven. Set the turkey in a roasting pan fitted with a rack.

3. In a small bowl, mix together the tapenade, olive oil, and orange zest. Take your hand and loosen the skin from the breast. Using a silicone spatula, spread the tapenade mixture under the skin of the turkey. Stuff the onion, scallions, and grapefruit into the cavity of the turkey. Drizzle olive oil all over the turkey and place in the oven.

4. Cook for about 30 minutes, and then reduce the oven temperature to 325°F. Continue cooking until a thermometer reads 165°F when inserted into the thickest part of the thigh, 3 to 3 ½ hours. Let the turkey rest for 20 to 30 minutes before carving.

Wild Rice Stuffing

Serves: 8   Skill Level: **Easy**   Prep Time: **30 minutes**   Cook Time: **45 minutes**

If you're used to boxed-stuffing mixes, get ready to have your mind blown. This stuffing recipe combines several textures (the softness of the bread, the crunchiness of the wild rice, the meatiness of the sausage) and flavors (the nuttiness of the rice, the sweetness of the sausage, and the savory taste of the veggies and herbs) that just belong together. I promise, once you make this stuffing (which is really easy to make, so don't be intimidated), you'll be thinking outside the box every Thanksgiving.

3 tablespoons olive oil

1 pound sweet Italian sausage, out of casing and crumbled

1 large white onion, small dice

1 cup carrots, small dice

1 cup celery, small dice

Salt and freshly ground black pepper, to taste

2 tablespoons thyme leaves

8 cups day-old white bread, cut into ½-inch cubes; toasted if not stale

½ cup butter, melted

3 cups raw wild rice, cooked according to package instructions

1 egg

2 cups chicken stock

1. Preheat oven to 375°F. Place a heavy-bottomed sauté pan over medium-high heat. Once hot, add olive oil and sausage. Brown the sausage evenly, then remove with a slotted spoon to a small bowl. Add the onion, carrots, and celery to the pan. Season with salt and pepper and cook until the vegetables are just tender, 3 to 4 minutes. Add more olive oil to the pan if it seems dry. Stir in the thyme once the vegetables are cooked.

2. In a large bowl, toss the day-old bread with the melted butter. Season with salt and pepper. Add the wild rice and cooked sausage and toss to combine. Add the sautéed vegetables and toss again. In a separate medium bowl, lightly beat the egg. Slowly whisk in the chicken stock, and once combined, pour the egg mixture over the bread mixture. Toss with your hands to thoroughly combine.

3. Transfer stuffing to a greased 9- x 13-inch baking dish. Bake in preheated oven for 20 to 30 minutes, or until the stuffing is golden brown and crunchy on top. Serve warm or at room temperature.

DAPHNE
When I throw a party, I try to adopt Carla's attitude that there are no mistakes. You've gotta roll with what happens and make sure to have fun no matter what!

Stuffed Acorn Squash

Serves: 12   Skill Level: **Moderate**   Prep Time: **30 minutes**   Cook Time: **1 hour, 10 minutes**

What's savory and sweet, chock-full of nutritious goodies, and a filling low-fat addition to the Thanksgiving menu? My stuffed acorn squash, of course. These gorgeous squash are bursting with color and can be served as a side for the whole crowd, or a main dish for the vegetarians in the house. Stuffed acorn squash is a feast for the eyes as well as the taste buds, which is, I think, how we should always approach preparing our food. This dish is a perfect example of bringing all five senses to bear when you're cooking: it looks great, smells wonderful, has varied textures, tastes amazing, and the moment your guests take their first bites, you'll hear them all say, "*Mmmmm!*"

4 ounces dried shiitake mushrooms

2 cups low-sodium vegetable stock

6 acorn squash, halved lengthwise and seeded

5 tablespoons butter, divided

½ cup maple syrup

1 large red onion, diced

Salt, to taste

2 carrots, peeled and diced

1 celery root, peeled and diced

Freshly ground black pepper

1 tablespoon thyme leaves

1 cup whole-wheat bread croutons, same size as diced vegetables

2 tart apples, peeled, cored, and diced

½ cup walnuts, toasted and chopped

¼ cup dried cranberries

1. Preheat oven to 350°F. Place the mushrooms and vegetable stock in a saucepot over medium-high heat and bring to a simmer. Steep the mushrooms until the liquid has been reduced by half. Remove from heat. Strain out the mushrooms and chop roughly. Reserve the stock.

2. Cut off a small part of the back of each acorn squash half so it sits flat on a parchment-lined baking sheet, with the hollow interior facing up. Heat 3 tablespoons butter and maple syrup together in a small pot just until butter melts. Stir and brush over the flesh of the squash.

3. Heat a large sauté pan over medium heat with remaining 2 tablespoons of butter. Sauté the onions for 2 minutes, seasoning with salt. Add the carrots and celery root and cook until softened, about 3 minutes. Season with salt and pepper, and add the thyme leaves.

4. Pour the vegetable mixture into a large bowl and toss with croutons, apples, walnuts, and cranberries. Add the mushrooms and stock, stirring to ensure liquid is absorbed by the croutons.

5. Divide the mixture among the hollows of the acorn squash halves, mounding but not overflowing. Cover with foil. Bake for 45 minutes, remove foil, and continue to cook for 15 minutes, or until the squash is fork-tender. Serve warm.

Pumpkin Pecan Pie

Serves: **8 to 10**   Skill Level: **Moderate**   Prep Time: **30 minutes**   Cook Time: **50 to 60 minutes**
Inactive Prep Time: **30 minutes**

You know how at the end of the Thanksgiving feast, you're sitting back, maybe secretly unbuttoning the top button of your pants and wishing you'd gone with elastic, and then someone pulls out a whole bunch of pies? That is a scary moment. Because you know you want some, but you're not going to be able to have more than just one slice without popping. Which do you choose? Classic pumpkin or classic pecan? *What do you do!?* No problem! Go for this pie that brings both of those favorites together and call it a day. The pumpkin pie lends its taste, body, and volume, and the pecan pie, with its sweetness and spice, delivers the BOOM BOOM BOOM! Mission accomplished.

FOR THE PIECRUST:

1 tablespoon sugar

½ teaspoon salt

⅓ cup water

1 cup cold, unsalted butter, cut into ½-inch pieces

2¼ cups flour (plus more for rolling)

FOR THE FILLING:

2 tablespoons butter, softened

½ cup granulated sugar

3 eggs, lightly beaten

1 tablespoon white vinegar

½ teaspoon salt

1 teaspoon vanilla extract

1 cup dark corn syrup

1½ cups pecans, chopped

¼ cup pumpkin puree

Whipped cream, for garnish

Cinnamon sugar, for garnish

TO MAKE THE PIECRUST:

1. In a small bowl, combine sugar, salt, and water. Refrigerate until very cold, about 15 minutes. During that time, refrigerate butter and flour.

2. Combine the cold butter and flour in the bowl of a food processor. Pulse until the butter and flour resemble wet sand, about 3 minutes. Add the water mixture all at once and pulse until the mixture just comes together.

3. Divide the dough in half and very gently pat each half into a round 1-inch-thick disk. Wrap each tightly in plastic wrap and refrigerate until firm, about 1 hour, before rolling. You can refrigerate the disks for up to one day or freeze for up to three months.

4. Preheat oven to 350°F. Roll out the pie dough to ⅛-inch thickness and transfer into a 9-inch pie plate, allowing the excess to drape over the edge. Fold over the edges and crimp, then trim any remaining excess. Cover crust with parchment paper and pour in baking beans or weights. Bake for 10 to 12 minutes, or until crust is light gold.

TO MAKE THE FILLING:

5. Meanwhile, in the bowl of an electric mixer, cream the butter and sugar, then add the beaten eggs, vinegar, salt, vanilla, and corn syrup. Stir in the pecans and pumpkin puree.

6. Pour the filling into the prepared piecrust. Place the pie on a baking sheet. Bake on the center rack of the oven for 40 to 50 minutes or until set. Cool completely on a wire rack. Garnish with whipped cream and cinnamon sugar.

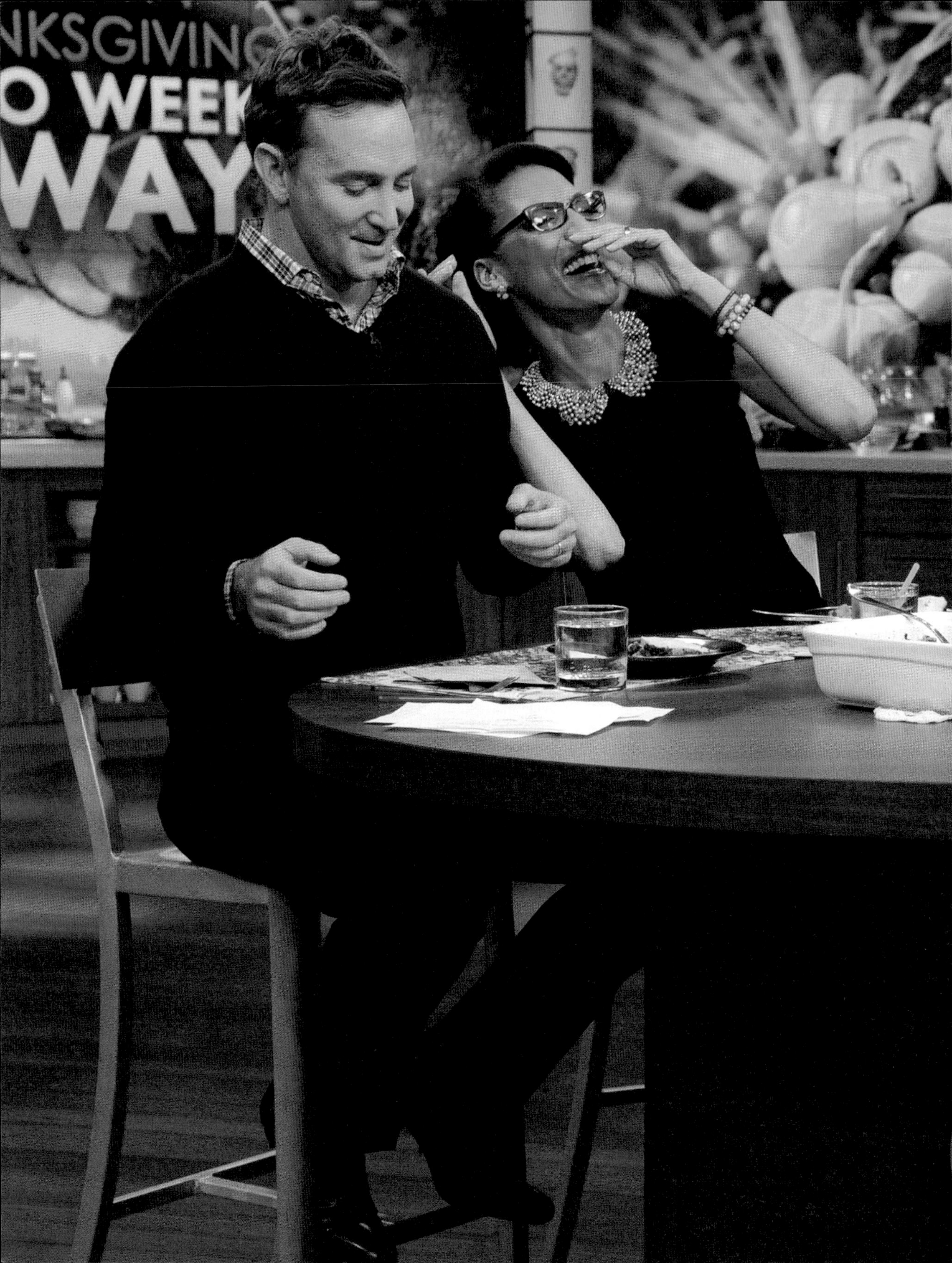
NKSGIVING
O WEEK
WAY

Leftover Turkey Soup

Serves: **6**   Skill Level: **Easy**   Prep Time: **20 to 25 minutes**   Cook Time: **1 hour, 15 minutes**

Thanksgiving is over and what do you have left? Among the fond memories and dishes that probably still need cleaning, you're likely to have a bunch of leftover turkey, as well as the bones (let's not say carcass . . . so unappetizing). The good news is that you have the makings for a fabulous soup that saves you from eating turkey sandwiches for the next month. Leftover turkey soup is easy to make, freezes well, and is a warming meal that's delicious and delightful to have on hand as the days get colder.

1½ pounds leftover cooked turkey bones

Water

Salt, to taste

3 tablespoons olive oil, plus more for drizzling

2 carrots, small chop

1 yellow onion, small chop

½ bunch kale, cut into ribbons

Freshly ground pepper, to taste

1 package egg noodles

1 baguette, thinly sliced on bias

½ cup freshly grated Parmesan, plus more for garnish

3 cups leftover shredded turkey

1. Preheat oven to broil. Place the turkey bones in a stockpot and cover with water by 2 inches. Bring to a boil and reduce to a simmer, cooking for 1 hour. Season with salt to taste. Remove the bones and strain the mixture, discarding solids.

2. In a large sauté pan over medium heat, heat oil and sauté the carrots, onion, and kale for 2 to 3 minutes. The vegetables should not be overly soft. Season to taste with salt and pepper. Remove from heat and set aside.

3. Bring a large pot of water to a boil and season with salt. Cook the egg noodles 2 minutes short of the package instructions. Drain.

4. Place the sliced bread on a baking sheet and drizzle with olive oil and sprinkle with ⅓ cup Parmesan. Broil for 2 minutes just until cheese has melted slightly. Divide the vegetable mixture and noodles among four bowls. Top with the shredded turkey. Ladle the turkey stock into each bowl and top with crostini and freshly grated Parmesan.

Glitter Pumpkin Tea Light Candleholders

The arrival of Thanksgiving might mean that Halloween is over, but it doesn't mean that you have to put your pumpkin-decorating skills on hold until next October. Little, teeny pumpkins (or any other small gourds) can be whittled away and sparkled up to do double duty as both table ornaments *and* functional candleholders. After you finish drilling and carving, get the kids out of their rooms, with all smartphones put away, and have a family free-for-all with glitter and glue. Cheap, fun, and glitzy . . . what more could you want in a candleholder?

Pumpkins

Electric drill with a 1½-inch hole saw attachment (or mallet and biscuit cutter)

Petroleum jelly

Newspaper

Craft glue

Bristle brush

Glitter

Tea light

1. Clear a work space and cover with newspaper. Clean the exterior of the pumpkin. For larger pumpkins, remove as much of the stem as you can using a knife or saw.

2. Center the hole saw over the remainder of the stem and drill down into the pumpkin, but don't push through. Let the tool do the work and then pull back the drill (this should take a few seconds). You can also use a mallet and a biscuit cutter to create the hole. Once you've drilled into the top of the pumpkin, scoop out or remove the circular piece. The hole you've created should be just the right size for a tea light to fit snugly inside. If the hole is too large, you can use a small piece of foil as a gasket to prevent the tea light from falling into the cavity of the pumpkin.

3. To keep the pumpkin from rotting too quickly, rub petroleum jelly around the inside edge of the hole.

4. Brush the outside of the pumpkin with craft glue using a bristle brush, ensuring that the pumpkin is completely coated with glue, but not dripping. With larger pumpkins, it may help to work in sections, while smaller pumpkins can be done all at once.

5. Pour glitter over the wet glue. Move and tilt the pumpkin to catch all the glitter. Continue until the surface is evenly covered.

6. Allow to sit for a few hours. If there are any bare spots once dry, repeat steps 4 and 5 until you have reached your desired results.

7. Once all glitter is dry, place a tea light in the center hole and enjoy the sparkle!

CHRISTMAS

Mistletoe Bellini

Serves: **1**   Skill Level: **Easy**   Prep Time: **10 minutes**

A traditional Bellini is a tantalizing mix of prosecco and peach puree, and originally hails from Harry's Bar in Venice, Italy. What we've done is taken the principle of a Bellini (pureed fruit and sparkling wine) and given it a Christmas twist by making it mistletoe red. The sprig of thyme adds that little bit of herbal greenery that helps to evoke the look of mistletoe. No need to go all the way to Venice to sip in splendor!

1 ounce fresh or frozen raspberries

1 ounce raspberry liqueur

4 ounces sparkling rosé

Thyme sprig

1. Blend raspberries in food processor to create the berry puree. Strain through fine-mesh sieve to remove seeds.

2. Combine puree, liqueur, and sparkling rosé in cocktail shaker with ice. Gently roll contents from one end of shaker to the other three times.

3. Strain into chilled champagne flute. Garnish with a sprig of thyme.

CLINTON
The rosy color of this cocktail lends itself to all sorts of other events and holidays as well. If plain old champagne feels tired on Valentine's Day, try whipping up a batch of these cocktails. Instead of calling them "Mistletoe Bellinis," why not "Beloved Bellinis"?

Fennel Pomegranate Crostini

Serves: 12   Skill Level: Easy   Prep Time: 15 minutes   Cook Time: 10 minutes

So many Christmas goodies can be a little on the heavy side. Which is, of course, part of why they're so delicious! But a dish with healthy ingredients that is gorgeous to look at and *tastes* just as gorgeous can happily coexist on your Christmas feast table. The light green fennel and ruby pomegranate seeds echo the traditional colors of this holiday and will, we think, become a staple for all your dinner parties.

1 baguette, sliced into half-inch pieces

2 cloves garlic, peeled

3 tablespoons extra-virgin olive oil

Juice and zest of 2 lemons

1 teaspoon hot red pepper flakes

1 jalapeño, seeded, stem removed, and sliced into rings

1 bulb fennel, core removed, shaved paper thin

2 ounces Pecorino pepato, shaved or grated

¼ cup pomegranate seeds

Salt and freshly ground pepper, to taste

1. Toast the crostini on a sheet tray in a 400°F oven until golden brown, about 10 minutes. Remove from the oven and rub each crostini with garlic.

2. In a large bowl, combine the olive oil, lemon juice and zest, hot red pepper flakes, jalapeño, fennel, Pecorino, and pomegranate seeds and toss everything to coat. Season with salt and freshly ground pepper. Mound on each crostini and serve.

Mario and Carla share their favorite wintry menus with Lenny Venito.

Roasted Pork Loin with Cranberries

Serves: **8**   Skill Level: **Moderate**   Prep Time: **30 minutes**   Cook Time: **55 minutes to 1 hour**

This is a perfect holiday main course. Why run around panicking, making a complicated dish, when you can assemble something that is not only tasty but easy peasy to make? We love this dish because once it's in the oven, you're free to hang out with your guests and enjoy their company. And once it's done, you have a juicy roast flavored with red cranberries and green apples—it couldn't be more Christmasy!

FOR THE PORK LOIN:

½ cup dried cranberries

1¼ cups cranberry juice, divided

3 tablespoons olive oil, plus more for rub

2 shallots, minced

¾ cup Granny Smith apples, medium dice

Salt and freshly ground black pepper, to taste

2 teaspoons fresh thyme leaves

2 teaspoons sage

¼ cup toasted walnuts, chopped

3 pounds boneless pork loin, fat cap left on; butterflied

1 cup red wine

3 tablespoons butter

1½ tablespoons Dijon mustard

TO MAKE THE PORK LOIN:

1. Preheat the oven to 450°F. Soak the cranberries in ¾ cup cranberry juice for 15 minutes.

2. Heat a large sauté pan over medium-high heat and add olive oil. Once hot, add the shallots, apples, cranberries, and remaining cranberry juice to the pan. Season with salt and pepper. Cook for 4 to 5 minutes, stirring occasionally, until apples have slightly softened. Continue to cook until the sauce has reduced by three quarters.

3. Remove from heat and toss in the fresh thyme and sage. Fold in the toasted walnuts, and then let the mixture cool.

4. Lay the butterflied pork loin on the cutting board with the fat cap facing down. Season generously with salt and pepper. Spoon the stuffing down the loin horizontally. Roll the pork over the stuffing, like a jelly roll, until the seam is facing down and the fat cap is on top. Tie the loin with twine at 1½-inch intervals. Rub the loin with olive oil, and season with salt and pepper. Place the loin in a roasting rack and put in the oven. Cook for 45 minutes. Turn the heat down to 325°F and continue cooking until internal temperature reads 140°F on a thermometer. Remove the roast from the pan and let rest for a minimum of 15 minutes.

FOR THE KALE:

4 tablespoons olive oil

6 garlic cloves, peeled

½ teaspoon chili flakes

2 bunches of kale, de-ribbed and chopped

2 tablespoons red wine vinegar

Salt and pepper to taste

SPECIAL EQUIPMENT:

Butcher's twine

5. Finish the sauce by putting the roasting pan on the stovetop over medium-high heat. Add the wine to the pan and let reduce by half. Add ½ cup of cranberry juice and scrape up all the bits on the bottom of the pan. Whisk in the butter, and then mix in the mustard. Adjust seasonings if necessary.

TO MAKE THE KALE:

6. While the pork is resting, heat a large, heavy-bottomed pan over medium-high heat. Add olive oil to the pan and toss in the garlic and chili flakes. Cook until soft, but do not allow to brown. Add in the kale and toss to coat. Reduce heat and let cook for about 15 minutes. Stir in the vinegar at the end, adjusting to taste.

7. Cut the twine off the pork and slice the roast in ½-inch slices. Serve with sauce and kale.

CARLA
Cranberries and pork are a perfect team because pork has a fatty, succulent flavor and texture, and tart cranberries cut right through that. The combination is a perfectly balanced taste sensation.

Sautéed Cipollini Onions

Serves: **6**   Skill Level: **Easy**   Prep Time: **30 minutes**   Cook Time: **18 to 20 minutes**

We are making cipollini onions three ways: simple; special, with robiolina cheese; and spectacular, with a mountain of shaved truffles. As foreign as cipollini onions may sound, they're not. They're just little onions; you could just as easily sub pearl onions for them. You can even use *frozen* pearl onions—no big deal. With all that said, if you can find cipollini onions, you'll find that they give you a little bit more resistance and a little bit more sweetness.

SIMPLE:

Olive oil

2 pounds cipollini onions, peeled with roots trimmed

Salt, to taste

1 tablespoon sugar

3 tablespoons unsalted butter

2 tablespoons fresh thyme leaves

1/3 cup sherry

1/4 cup heavy cream

SPECIAL:

1/2 cup robiolina or cream cheese

1/4 cup freshly grated Parmesan

SPECTACULAR:

Black or white truffles, shaved

TO MAKE IT SIMPLE:

1. Heat a large skillet over medium-high heat with a few tablespoons of olive oil. Add onions, and season with salt. Sprinkle the onions all over with sugar. Cook, undisturbed for 1 minute, and then add the butter, continuing to cook until the onions begin to develop deep caramelization, 5 to 8 minutes. Flip the onions, and cook for 1 minute, and then add the thyme, followed by the sherry. Cook for 10 minutes until sherry has reduced by 90 percent. Remove from heat and stir in the cream. Adjust seasoning to taste.

TO MAKE IT SPECIAL:

2. Stir in the robiolina and Parmesan.

TO MAKE IT SPECTACULAR:

3. Shave truffles over the onions, and then sprinkle the truffles with salt.

MARIO
What you're looking for in a perfectly cooked onion is a firm, al dente texture. It's very much like pasta. So, you want to cook your onions all the way through, but not until they're mushy.

Spicy Broccoli and Cauliflower Gratin

Serves: 10   Skill Level: Easy   Prep Time: 15 minutes   Cook Time: 40 to 45 minutes

Your Christmas table will be so happy if you have this side dish snuggling up to your turkey, ham, or whatever the main attraction happens to be. Not one, not two, but *three* cheeses and a crunchy bread-crumb topping make this gratin the comfort food to end all comfort foods. But before you get *too* comfortable, red chili flakes add a kick that will have you up from your chair looking for another serving.

3 tablespoons olive oil

1 medium yellow onion, diced

Salt, to taste

1 tablespoon chili powder

½ cup unsalted butter, divided, plus more as needed

4 tablespoons all-purpose flour

1 cup milk

1 cup heavy cream

½ pound Gruyère cheese, shredded

½ pound cheddar cheese, shredded

¼ cup freshly grated Parmesan

2 cups broccoli florets

2 cups cauliflower florets

1½ cups panko bread crumbs

Freshly ground black pepper, to taste

Red chili flakes

1. Preheat oven to 400°F. In a medium sauté pan, heat olive oil over medium heat. Sauté the onions until translucent, about 3 minutes. Season with salt and chili powder. Remove from heat and set aside.

2. Melt 4 tablespoons of butter with flour in a saucepot over medium heat. Stir together to form a dry paste and cook for 2 minutes. Slowly whisk in the milk and cream. Cook over medium heat for 5 minutes or until slightly thickened. Remove the sauce from the heat, and stir in the cheeses until melted. Add the cooked onions and adjust seasoning to taste.

3. Toss the broccoli and cauliflower in a 9- x 13-inch baking dish, making sure vegetables are mixed evenly. Pour the cheese sauce evenly over the vegetables. In a large bowl, toss together the bread crumbs and a splash of olive oil until bread is evenly coated. Season with the chili flakes, salt, and pepper.

4. Top the vegetable mix with the bread crumbs and bake for 30 to 35 minutes or until topping is rich gold in color. Remove from oven and allow to cool for 5 to 10 minutes before serving.

King of Greens Salad

Serves: 4   Skill Level: **Easy**   Prep Time: **15 minutes**

"The King of Kings salvation brings," or so says the traditional Christmas carol "What Child Is This?" In keeping with the spirit of the holiday, we bring you the "King of Greens." The King of Greens Salad is the ultimate in healthy and delicious eating. Some of you may think that kale is too fibrous to eat raw in a salad, but it's not true! All you've got to do is give it a good massage with the dressing to break the fibers down. That massage not only gives the kale a lovely texture, but it also helps the king of greens to absorb the dressing. Make friends with kale!

1 large bunch black kale, leaves torn into bite-sized pieces

Salt and freshly ground black pepper, to taste

¼ cup olive oil

Zest and juice of 1–2 lemons

⅓ cup currants

⅓ cup pine nuts, toasted

¼ cup Pecorino, grated

1 teaspoon red chili flakes, optional

1. Add the kale to a large mixing bowl, season with salt and pepper, and drizzle with olive oil. Massage with your hands making sure to coat the kale with oil and begin to break down the cell structure.

2. Grate the zest and squeeze the juice of the lemons over the massaged kale. Add the currants, toasted pine nuts, and Pecorino and toss to combine. Serve with a pinch of red chili flakes, if desired.

DAPHNE
K is for kale. It's also for vitamin K. All green vegetables are rich in vitamins and minerals *and* have proven anti-inflammatory properties.

Sticky Toffee Pudding

Serves: 6   Skill Level: Moderate   Prep Time: 15 minutes   Cook Time: 30 minutes

You don't have to be British to love this English dessert. But don't let the name confuse you! The Brits call their "French fries" *chips*, they say *lift* instead of "elevator," and they use the word *pudding* when talking about any type of dessert. So this isn't a creamy cup of custard; it's actually a cake smothered in warm, sugary, buttery goodness. If you've got a little time on your hands and want to wow your guests as well as yourself, this one's for you.

FOR THE CAKE:

1¼ cups pitted dates, cut crosswise into ¼-inch slices

¾ cup hot water

1¼ cups all-purpose flour

½ teaspoon baking soda

½ teaspoon baking powder

½ teaspoon salt

4 tablespoons unsalted butter, softened

¾ cup packed dark brown sugar

1½ teaspoons vanilla extract

2 large eggs

¼ teaspoon lemon zest

Vanilla ice cream, whipped cream, or Greek yogurt, to serve

FOR THE TOFFEE SAUCE:

8 tablespoons unsalted butter

1 cup dark brown sugar

1⅔ cups heavy cream

Pinch of salt

1 tablespoon dark rum

TO MAKE THE CAKE:

1. Preheat oven to 350°F. Grease and flour 6, ½-cup ramekins and set aside.

2. Combine the dates and hot water in a bowl. Cover with plastic wrap and allow the dates to soften, about 15 minutes. Puree date/water mixture in a blender and cool. Place the flour, baking soda, baking powder, and salt on parchment or wax paper. This will make it easy to pour the flour mixture into the stand mixer. Set aside.

3. In the bowl of an electric mixer, cream the butter and brown sugar until light and fluffy. Add the vanilla, eggs, zest, and date puree. Fold the parchment paper with the dry ingredients in half and pour into the stand mixer. Divide batter into prepared ramekins, place ramekins on a baking sheet, and bake about 20 minutes. Cool slightly and remove the cakes from the ramekins. Serve with the warm sauce and your choice of ice cream, whipped cream, or yogurt.

TO MAKE THE TOFFEE SAUCE:

4. In a heavy saucepan over medium heat, combine the butter, brown sugar, 1 cup of the heavy cream, and salt. Cook, stirring often, for 10 minutes, or until the sugar is completely dissolved and the mixture is smooth.

5. Stir in the rum and remaining ⅔ cup heavy cream. Spoon over cakes and serve.

Rum Balls

Serves: 24   Skill Level: **Easy**   Prep Time: **30 to 45 minutes**   Cook Time: **10 minutes**

Looking for a traditional Christmas treat? Look no further than the classic rum ball! Let's face it, if you add rum to chocolate and butter it's pretty hard to go wrong. The addition of a little salt to offset the sweetness of these confections is what takes them from great to GREAT! And if you have a hankering for another liquor, go right ahead and make the change. If bourbon is your thing, swap it in for the rum. Or use red and green sprinkles to decorate them. Make this recipe your own!

¼ cup dark rum

6 ounces semisweet chocolate, chopped

4 tablespoons butter

¼ cup walnuts, toasted and finely chopped

1½ cups powdered sugar

Salt, to taste

White sprinkles, for decorating

1. Heat the rum in a small skillet over medium heat until reduced by half. Set aside.

2. Set a heatproof bowl over a pot of gently simmering water, making sure that the bowl does not touch the surface of the water. Add chocolate and butter to the bowl and melt, stirring to combine.

3. Remove from heat and stir in the walnuts, rum, powdered sugar, and salt until fully incorporated. Allow mixture to cool to room temperature. This can also be prepared a few days in advance and stored, covered in the fridge.

4. Portion dough into one-inch balls and roll in sprinkles. Chill in an airtight container until ready to serve.

Hot Cocoa Mix

Christmas comes during the season of giving, so when you are going to a Christmas party or a family gathering, it's always nice to bring a gift with you. Especially a homemade one! This hot cocoa mix is simple to put together, and you can make a big batch to give to all your loved ones! Simply pour it into glass jars, make little direction cards that say "Combine 2 tablespoons of mix with hot milk," punch a hole in the corner of each card, and tie around the neck of the jar with festive colored ribbons! Ho! Ho! Ho! Or should I say, "Cocoa-oh!"

1 cup cocoa powder

2 teaspoons ground cardamom

2 teaspoons ground chipotle powder

2 teaspoons ground cinnamon

3 tablespoons semisweet chocolate chips, chopped

½ cup sugar

Glass jar with lid

Blank index card or gift tag

Hole puncher

Festive ribbon

1. Mix ingredients thoroughly and transfer to a jar. Top with lid.

2. On a blank index card or gift tag, write, "To prepare, mix 2 tablespoons of the mix into 8 ounces hot milk." Punch a hole in the corner of the index card and thread onto a piece of ribbon roughly a foot long. Tie ribbon in a bow around the neck of the jar.

HANUKKAH

Chicken Liver Pâté

Serves: **5**   Skill Level: **Easy**   Prep Time: **10 minutes**   Cook Time: **15 minutes**

Since Hanukkah is the Festival of Lights, let's shed some light on the topic of chopped liver. It is a traditional Jewish dish, but let's face it: it doesn't sound all that fancy. In fact, it's an expression used by a person who is feeling underappreciated: "What am I? Chopped liver?" With this recipe, we are taking a hint from the fabulous French and whipping the classic holiday dish into a non-dairy pâté. Enjoy it on crackers, with toast, or just eat it with a spoon!

2 tablespoons olive oil

½ cup finely chopped yellow onion

1 clove garlic, minced

1 cup chicken livers, finely chopped

2 teaspoons chopped parsley

2 teaspoons chopped sage

¼ cup sherry

½ teaspoon salt

½ teaspoon pepper

1. Heat the olive oil over medium heat in a medium-sized skillet. Add the onion and sauté until translucent. Add the garlic, chicken livers, parsley, and sage. Stir until the liver is cooked through, about 10 minutes.

2. Increase the heat to high, add the sherry, and cook for 3 more minutes. Add salt and pepper.

3. Remove from the heat and pulse in a food processor until blended. The final mixture should be a little chunky. Chill and serve with crostini or crackers.

CLINTON
I've picked up so much from all of the other hosts. It's not just one recipe but the spirit with which they cook that's really affected me.

Brisket with Pearl Onions and Potatoes

Serves: 6 to 8   Skill Level: Easy   Prep Time: 20 minutes   Cook Time: 2 ½ to 3 hours

Brisket is a Jewish holiday classic, hands down. You think "Hanukkah," you think "brisket." You think "Passover," you think "brisket." The excitement enters the picture when you decide how you're going to prepare it. Everyone swears that their bubbe's brisket is the best. That may be; I'm not going to argue with anyone's bubbe. But I think this brisket could very well give those grandes dames a run for their gelt.

4- to 5-pound brisket

Salt and freshly ground black pepper

3 tablespoons olive oil

½ pound pearl onions

1 tablespoon tomato paste

8 cloves garlic

1 bay leaf

4 sprigs rosemary, tied in a bundle

6 carrots, peeled and cut into 2-inch chunks

6 parsnips, peeled and cut into 2-inch chunks

2 pounds Yukon Gold potatoes

2 tablespoons flour

1 cup red wine

3 cups beef stock

Fresh horseradish, to garnish, optional

1. Preheat oven to 300°F. Season the brisket generously with salt and pepper. Heat a large Dutch oven over medium-high heat. Add olive oil and sear the brisket deeply on all sides, about 5 minutes per side. Remove to a plate.

2. Add the onions to the remaining hot oil and cook for 2 minutes. Add the tomato paste and cook until it begins to turn a rusty color, then add the garlic, bay leaf, and rosemary. Add the vegetables and flour and toss with a wooden spoon to lightly coat the vegetables in the flour and tomato mixture. Add the wine to deglaze the pan, scraping the brown bits off of the bottom of the pan with a wooden spoon as much as possible. Add the brisket back to the pan and add stock to come one third of the way up the side of the pan.

3. Cover and transfer to oven and cook 2 to 3 hours, until meat is very tender. Garnish with freshly grated horseradish.

Beet and Potato Pancakes

Serves: **6**   Skill Level: **Easy**   Prep Time: **20 minutes**   Cook Time: **4 to 8 minutes**

Potato pancakes, or latkes, are a Hanukkah staple. Normally, they're served with a choice of savory or sweet condiments; in other words, applesauce or sour cream. These potato pancakes are a little fancier but don't require any more work and are just as delicious, if not more so, than the original. The addition of beets adds an unexpected splash of color on your plate as well as a little sweetness to the pancake; and we give a dash of *chutzpah* to the traditional sour cream garnish by adding horseradish. The horseradish is a perfect foil to the sweet beets and goes perfectly with beef, which also usually shows up on the Hanukkah table.

FOR THE LATKES:

2 large red beets, peeled

1 medium yellow onion

1 egg

2 medium russet potatoes, peeled

¼ teaspoon baking powder

2 tablespoons flour

1 teaspoon salt

¼ teaspoon freshly ground black pepper

4 tablespoons butter or olive oil, plus more as needed

2 scallions, chopped, plus more for garnish

FOR THE HORSERADISH SOUR CREAM:

1 cup sour cream

2 tablespoons freshly grated horseradish, plus more for garnish

2 teaspoons Dijon mustard

1 tablespoon chopped scallions

Salt and freshly ground black pepper, to taste

TO MAKE THE LATKES:

1. Grate the beets and onions onto a clean kitchen towel. Wring out the excess liquid and place in a large mixing bowl. Crack the egg into the bowl. Rinse the grater and then grate the potatoes onto a clean kitchen towel. Wring out the excess liquid and place in the bowl with the beets and onions. In a medium bowl, whisk together the baking powder, flour, salt, and pepper. Add the flour mixture to the beet mixture and stir to incorporate.

2. Heat a large sauté pan over medium heat and melt butter until the foam subsides. Using a tablespoon, spoon the beet mixture into the pan, making sure not to overcrowd. Using the back of the spoon, press the mixture in the pan to flatten slightly. Cook for 2 minutes or until crispy on the first side and then flip to continue cooking. Once crispy on both sides, remove to a paper towel–lined plate. Continue to cook the remaining beet mix, cleaning the pan to remove burnt bits and adding butter or oil as needed.

3. Serve the pancakes with a dollop of the horseradish sour cream and a sprinkling of scallions and more freshly grated horseradish.

TO MAKE THE HORSERADISH SOUR CREAM:

4. Mix together the ingredients in a bowl and adjust seasoning to taste.

The Chew: A Year of Celebrations

Kugel

Serves: 8 to 10   Skill Level: **Easy**   Prep Time: **30 minutes**   Cook Time: **45 to 60 minutes**

Kugel is a little bit like the Talmud. It raises more questions than it answers. Is it a pudding? Not really. Is it a casserole? Not so much. Is it sweet? Umm . . . sort of. Is it savory? Uhhh . . . kinda. Okay, enough with the questions. Here's what we can say about kugel: it's hard to find someone who doesn't like it, and if you're hungry in the middle of the night, this is the perfect thing to snack on right out of the refrigerator.

- 4 matzo crackers
- ½ cup water
- 1 cup sherry
- ¾ cup golden raisins
- 6 eggs
- ½ cup maple syrup
- ½ teaspoon salt
- ¼ teaspoon cinnamon
- ¾ cup almonds, crushed
- 2 Granny Smith apples, shredded
- 4 tablespoons melted butter
- ½ cup orange juice
- 1 cup apricot jam

1. Preheat oven to 350°F. Soak the matzo crackers in water for 10 minutes. Remove from the water with a slotted spoon and allow any excess moisture to drip off. Set aside.

2. In a small saucepan over medium heat, add the sherry and raisins. Cook for 3 to 5 minutes until the raisins have absorbed the wine and become plump. When the raisins are plump, remove from the sherry with a slotted spoon and set aside.

3. Whisk together the matzo and the eggs in a large bowl. Add the maple syrup, salt, cinnamon, and almonds. Fold in the apples, raisins, melted butter, and orange juice. Pour into a greased 9- x 9-inch baking dish. Cook, covered with foil, for 35 to 45 minutes until just set. Remove the pan from the oven and spread apricot jam on top. Return to oven, uncovered, and cook for another 10 to 15 minutes.

MICHAEL
Kugel is special not only because it's so addictively good, but it does double duty. It's a classic Hanukkah, Passover, and Sabbath dish, *and* it is a traditional everyday food in Romania. This puts kugel in the good company of stuffed cabbage and goulash.

Potato Doughnuts

Serves: **10**   Skill Level: **Moderate**   Prep Time: **15 minutes**   Cook Time: **50 minutes**

Inactive Cook Time: **1 hour**

Make no mistake—we're not saying that Hanukkah fare is particularly light and healthy. But who cares? It happens once a year, so if you subscribe to the notion of "all things in moderation," you're in good shape. These potato doughnuts are tender as can be and flavored with a little kick of vermouth and orange. Delectable and irresistible, they disappear faster than you can say *menorah*!

½ pound russet potatoes, peeled and cut into chunks

½ cup whole milk

2 teaspoons active dry yeast

2 large eggs

3½–4 cups all-purpose flour (or as needed)

1½ teaspoons salt

2 tablespoons sugar

¼ cup extra-virgin olive oil (plus 4 cups for deep-frying)

2 tablespoons sweet red vermouth

Grated zest and juice of 1 orange

Granulated sugar, for dusting

1. Place the potatoes in a large pot, cover with water, and bring to a boil. Boil gently until tender. Drain and pass through a food mill or ricer into a large bowl. Let cool.

2. Meanwhile, in a small saucepan, heat the milk over low heat just until warm. Remove from the heat, sprinkle the yeast into the milk, and let sit for 15 minutes, or until foamy. Add the eggs, flour, salt, sugar, ¼ cup olive oil, vermouth, and orange zest and juice to the potatoes and mix well to combine. Add the yeast mixture and knead well, adding a little more flour if necessary if the dough is very sticky. Cover and let the dough rise in a warm place for 1 hour, or until doubled.

3. Divide the dough into four equal pieces. Roll each one into a 1½-inch thick rope. Cut each one into 5-inch lengths and form into rings. Place the doughnuts on a well-oiled baking sheet, cover with a towel, and let rise for 45 minutes, or until doubled.

4. In a deep pot, heat the remaining 4 cups olive oil to 340°F. Working in batches, fry the doughnuts until golden brown, about 5 minutes per batch. Remove with a slotted spoon and drain on a plate lined with paper towels. Sprinkle generously with granulated sugar while hot and serve warm.

MARIO
If you really want to stay away from fried foods, you can bake these doughnuts. They won't be as crispy, but that doesn't matter; they'll still be sweetly satisfying.

Homemade Hanukkah Gelt

Dreidel, dreidel, dreidel, I made you out of clay . . . and then I let you dry and spun you like a top to do a little homegrown gambling! Never fear, this isn't the kind of gambling to get worried about. No money changes hands, unless you count chocolates wrapped in foil as money. If so, you're my kind of person. Here's how you do it:

2 cups dark chocolate chips

½ teaspoon vanilla extract

Aluminum foil

2 mini-muffin tins

1. Set a heatproof bowl over a pot of gently simmering water, making sure that the bowl does not touch the surface of the water. Add the chocolate chips and the vanilla extract, stirring constantly until chips are completely melted, about 5 minutes.

2. Transfer the chocolate to a pitcher. Pour chocolate into the wells of mini-muffin tins so that chocolate is about ⅛-inch deep in the bottom of each well.

3. Place the mini-muffin tins in the fridge, and allow the gelt to harden for at least 1 hour. Once chilled, wrap in foil if desired, or store in an airtight container.

VALENTINE'S DAY

Gin Fizz

Serves: 1   Skill Level: **Easy**   Prep Time: **3 minutes**

Frankly, gin fizzes are good any time of the year, particularly in the summertime, as they are cooling, elegant, old-school cocktails. But if you want a little bubbly for Valentine's Day and want to try something off the beaten path, a gin fizz is your drink. As sweet as your love, as sparkly as your time together, and a little bit tart (I'm not even going to touch that one), a gin fizz is right on for celebrating the day of love.

FOR THE SIMPLE SYRUP:

1 cup granulated sugar

1 cup water

FOR THE GIN FIZZ:

3 ounces gin

2 ounces fresh lemon juice

1 ounce simple syrup

5 ounces soda water

TO MAKE THE SIMPLE SYRUP:

1. Place the sugar and the water in a small saucepan and bring to a boil. Cook until the sugar has dissolved, about 5 minutes. Cool and store in an airtight container for up to two weeks. Makes 1 cup simple syrup.

TO MAKE THE GIN FIZZ:

2. Combine gin, lemon juice, and simple syrup in a drink shaker with ice. Shake and strain into a highball glass over two ice cubes.

3. Fill with carbonated water, stir, and serve.

CLINTON
Sure, chocolate and flowers are nice. But they don't exactly say that you put a ton of thought into your gift. To really make an impact, think of something that symbolizes your relationship.

Curried Butternut Squash Soup

Serves: 4   Skill Level: **Easy**   Prep Time: **15 minutes**   Cook Time: **25 minutes**

Why curried butternut squash soup for Valentine's Day, you ask? Why not a red soup, like borscht or tomato, to go with the usual red-and-white theme? Get ready for greatness: because curry is known to be an aphrodisiac and mood enhancer. You read that right. The spicy heat in curry releases endorphins, the feel-good chemical, in your body, and the other ingredients are believed to get you heated up in other ways. Ginger, garlic, cardamom, and ginseng all make appearances in most curries and are responsible for getting your motor running. Why are you still reading this? Start making soup!

2 tablespoons olive oil

2 tablespoons unsalted butter, divided

4 cups butternut squash, peeled, seeded, and cut into ½-inch cubes

1 small yellow onion, diced

Pinch salt, plus more to taste

1, 2-inch piece ginger, peeled and finely grated

2 teaspoons curry powder or curry paste

1, 15-ounce can coconut milk

1 cup water

Freshly ground black pepper, to taste

Cilantro leaves, for garnish

Lime wedges, for garnish

Plain Greek yogurt, for garnish

Toasted butternut squash seeds, for garnish

1. Preheat oven to 350°F. In a Dutch oven, heat the olive oil and butter over medium-high heat. Add the butternut squash, onion, and a generous pinch of salt, and sauté until softened. Add the ginger and the curry powder or paste and cook until very fragrant, about a minute. Add the coconut milk and water, and bring to a simmer. (Do not overheat. Boiling will cause the coconut milk to break down.) Cook for 15 minutes to allow flavors to come together.

2. Use blender to puree the soup until completely smooth. Check seasonings, adjusting with salt and pepper. Ladle the soup into bowls. Garnish with croutons, cilantro, lime wedges, yogurt, and toasted seeds.

Scallops with Slow-Roasted Cauliflower Steak

Serves: **4 to 6**   Skill Level: **Moderate**   Prep Time: **15 minutes**   Cook Time: **10 minutes**

Surf and turf, while a nice idea, can be a little overwhelming both for your stomach and your wallet. This take on the classic marriage actually involves "steak" made with cauliflower! It is just as tempting as the original but nowhere near the cost. And you won't pay the price with your waistline either. If you love scallops, give this a try; you probably don't already know how perfectly matched cauliflower and scallops are, but you'll be setting them up on a date again after eating this dish.

6 tablespoons extra-virgin olive oil, divided

1 small head cauliflower, cut into ½-inch-thick slices

Salt and freshly ground black pepper, to taste

1 teaspoon minced white anchovy

2 tablespoons capers, rinsed

1 small shallot, minced

1 garlic clove, minced

1 tablespoon honey

Juice and zest of 1 lemon

Juice and zest of 1 orange

1 pound sea scallops, approximately 16

¼ cup pine nuts, toasted

¼ cup fresh parsley, leaves only

1. Preheat broiler to high with a rack positioned 6 inches below heat. In a large sauté pan over medium-high heat, add 1 tablespoon of olive oil. Once very hot, arrange the cauliflower in the pan and sauté until it begins to caramelize, about a minute. Season generously with salt and pepper. Transfer the pan to the oven under the broiler and cook until browned on the top, 4 to 5 minutes, being mindful not to burn. Remove from oven and set aside.

2. In a medium bowl, combine the anchovy, capers, shallot, garlic, honey, and lemon and orange juices and zest. Whisk in 3 tablespoons of olive oil and season with salt and freshly ground black pepper. Set aside.

3. Place a large sauté pan over high heat. Remove the small side muscle from the scallops and pat them dry with paper towels. Season on both sides with salt. When the pan is hot, add 2 tablespoons of olive oil and add the scallops, with enough space in between to allow browning. Sear without moving them for about 1 minute to 90 seconds on the first side. There should be a golden-brown crust, while the scallop is still translucent throughout. Turn the heat off and flip scallops. Let the scallops sit in the pan while you plate the cauliflower.

4. To serve, arrange cauliflower and scallops on plates or a platter. Drizzle with the vinaigrette and garnish with pine nuts and parsley.

PAGES 126–127: On Valentine's Day, country music group Little Big Town (Jimi Westbrook, Karen Fairchild, Kimberly Schlapman, and Philip Sweet) have a heart-to-heart with *The Chew* crew.

Coq au Vin

Serves: 6 to 8   Skill Level: **Easy**   Prep Time: **15 minutes**   Cook Time: **1 hour, 45 minutes**

Valentine's Day is about love, and who knows more about love than the French? Well, maybe Italians, but I won't quibble today. In honor of the day of love and the people who invented the French kiss, you can't go wrong making coq au vin to share with your sweetheart. It's the perfect dish for Valentine's Day because once all the ingredients go in the pot, you've got two hours to dress up (or down) at your leisure before your guest of honor arrives. When the coq au vin hits the table and you hear your honey repeating the word "love" a lot, you can be sure it's meant both for you and this incredible dish.

3 tablespoons extra-virgin olive oil

6 ounces pancetta (½-inch dice)

1, 4-pound chicken, cut into 8 pieces; wings and back reserved for stock

Salt

2 carrots, small dice

2 celery ribs, small dice

5 cipollini onions or pearl onions, trimmed

3 garlic cloves, thinly sliced

1 cup cremini or button mushrooms, halved

Salt and freshly ground black pepper, to taste

3 tablespoons tomato paste

Flour, for dusting

1 cup chicken stock

4 cups red wine, reduced to 3 cups; preferably cabernet or merlot

6 fresh thyme sprigs

6 fresh parsley sprigs

1. Heat olive oil in a large Dutch oven over medium heat. Add the pancetta and cook until browned on all sides. Remove from pan. Add the chicken in batches and brown on all sides, starting skin-side down, until golden. Remove to a plate.

2. Add the carrots, celery, onion, garlic, and mushrooms to the pan and sauté until softened slightly, about 5 minutes, seasoning with salt and pepper. Add the tomato paste and cook until dark rust in color. Sprinkle in 1 to 2 tablespoons of flour just to coat vegetables.

3. Pour in the chicken stock and reduced wine. Tie the herbs into a bundle with kitchen twine and add to pot along with the browned chicken and pancetta. Bring to a boil and reduce to a simmer. Cover and cook for 1½ hours. Serve warm over mashed potatoes or buttered noodles.

MARIO
The liquid used to braise the chicken can be used for any kind of meat. Let your imagination run wild! Or if you've got a cut of meat and don't know what you're going to do with it, remember this classic that won't let you down.

Glazed Gingersnaps

Serves: **Makes 3 dozen**   Skill Level: **Easy**   Prep Time: **10 minutes**   Cook Time: **10 to 15 minutes**

Hey! Here are our friends cardamom and ginger again, putting gingersnaps in the unlikely category of aphrodisiac! Who knew? These classic cookies are a spicy and unexpectedly sexy treat that I've made a little more health conscious. The usual suspects of eggs and butter are replaced with applesauce and coconut oil. And I use maple syrup instead of brown or white sugar, which is a natural way to sweeten baked treats. Plus, maple syrup is loaded with antioxidants and nutrients, and the maple flavor blends irresistibly with the spices in these snaps. It's a match made in cookie heaven!

FOR THE GLAZE:

½ cup confectioners' sugar

¼ teaspoon cardamom

Juice of 1 lemon

FOR THE COOKIES:

2½ cups unbleached flour

1½ teaspoons baking soda

½ teaspoon ground cinnamon

½ teaspoon ground ginger

½ teaspoon cardamom

Salt

¼ cup real maple syrup

¾ cup coconut oil (measured while solid, then melted)

¼ cup unsweetened natural applesauce

¼ cup molasses

1 tablespoon freshly grated ginger

TO MAKE THE GLAZE:

1. In a small bowl, mix together the confectioners' sugar, cardamom, and lemon juice. Mix until liquid, adding a small amount more water if necessary.

TO MAKE THE COOKIES:

2. Preheat oven to 350°F. In a medium bowl, whisk together the flour, baking soda, cinnamon, ground ginger, cardamom, and salt.

3. In a large bowl, using an electric mixer or a whisk, combine the maple syrup, coconut oil, applesauce, molasses, and fresh ginger. Gradually add in the dry mixture until the dough comes together. Form into 1-inch balls and arrange on a cookie sheet, evenly spaced.

4. Bake for 10 to 12 minutes, until very dark, rotating halfway through cook time. Cool on a wire rack, and use a pastry brush to lightly glaze.

Espresso Crème Brûlée

Serves: **4**   Skill Level: **Moderate**   Prep Time: **25 minutes**   Cook Time: **20 to 25 minutes**
Inactive Cook Time: **30 minutes**

Ah, love. It makes us say crazy things and do even crazier stuff. And why does that happen? Because we lose our damned fool minds, that's why! And how do we describe how we feel when we're crazy in love? We say that we are feverish, our hearts are aflame, or that the object of our affection has set us on fire. If that's how you're feeling, show your honey some sweet love by serving up this espresso crème brûlée. He or she will get the hint; in French, *brûlée* means "set on fire." Case closed!

1 cup heavy cream

½ cup whole milk

2 tablespoons coarsely ground espresso beans

2 teaspoons instant espresso powder

1 vanilla bean, split

6 egg yolks

6 tablespoons granulated sugar

¼ teaspoon salt

¼ cup raw (turbinado) sugar

1. In a 3-quart pot combine heavy cream, whole milk, espresso beans, espresso powder, and vanilla bean. Heat over medium heat until the mixture starts to boil, then immediately remove from heat. Set aside and let steep for 5 minutes. Stir and strain through a fine-mesh strainer. In a separate bowl, whisk together the egg yolks, sugar, and salt until lemon yellow. Slowly drizzle the hot milk mixture into the egg mixture and stir quickly until combined and sugar is dissolved. Pour the mixture into four, 8-ounce ramekins.

2. Preheat oven to 425°F. Place a kitchen towel in the bottom of a roasting pan, and then place the ramekins in the pan. Place the pan in the oven and pour hot water halfway up the sides of the ramekins. Bake for 20 to 25 minutes, until custard jiggles or is just set. Remove from pan and refrigerate for 2 hours.

3. When ready to serve, let custards sit at least 30 minutes at room temperature, then dust tops of custard with 1 teaspoon raw (turbinado) sugar. Place under broiler for 2 to 3 minutes or use a kitchen torch to brown. Be careful not to burn the tops.

EASTER

Moscow Mule

Serves: **1**   Skill Level: **Easy**   Prep Time: **5 minutes**

What can we say about a Moscow mule? The ingredients are pretty straightforward. Frankly, you've gotta love a recipe that only has three ingredients, right? So during the three seconds that it takes to put this cocktail together, remember that this tasty drink can go down like soda, but drink it slowly; all that (Moscow) vodka gives it a kick like a mule!

½ ounce lime juice

2 ounces vodka

4 to 6 ounces ginger beer

1. Pour the lime juice into a collins glass. Add ice cubes, then add the vodka.

2. Fill the rest of the glass with ginger beer.

MICHAEL
I have no idea how the Greek calendar works. All I know is that when I was a kid it was great because I got to celebrate Easter twice!

Chickpea Bruschetta with Spring Vegetable Salad

Serves: **6 to 8**   Skill Level: **Easy**   Prep Time: **30 minutes**   Cook Time: **2 to 4 minutes**

Bruschetta, which is pronounced "broo-SKET-a," comes from the past participle of the verb *bruscare*, which means to cook over open coals. You don't have to use open coals; you can just as easily use a grill pan or a toaster oven. All you really need is some nice crusty bread and anything you want to put on top of it. It could easily be leftovers from the night before, or any veggie that's in season. Garbanzos are one of my heroes, and I always keep them in my pantry.

FOR THE CHICKPEA BRUSCHETTA:

2, 15-ounce cans chickpeas, rinsed and drained

1 tablespoon black olive paste

¼ cup extra-virgin olive oil

½ large red onion, halved lengthwise and thinly sliced

Pinch hot red pepper flakes

Flaky sea salt

6, 1-inch slices of crusty bread, such as filone or baguette

2 garlic cloves, peeled

FOR THE SPRING VEGETABLE SALAD:

2 cups asparagus, sliced into thin rounds

1 cup carrots, sliced into thin rounds

½ cup radishes, stems cleaned and shaved thinly

¾ cup peas, shelled

Salt and freshly ground black pepper, to taste

TO MAKE THE CHICKPEA BRUSCHETTA:

1. Preheat a grill to medium-high or an oven broiler. In a mixing bowl, gently stir together the chickpeas, black olive paste, olive oil, onion, and red pepper flakes, and then season with the flaky sea salt. Taste and adjust seasoning.

2. Grill or broil each slice of bread until lightly toasted, about 2 minutes per side. Rub the surface of the bread with the garlic. Spoon the chickpea mixture onto each of the grilled bread slices, making sure to use the liquid in the bottom of the bowl, and serve immediately.

TO MAKE THE SPRING VEGETABLE SALAD:

3. Combine all of the vegetables in a mixing bowl and season with salt and pepper.

4. In a medium bowl combine the tarragon, Dijon mustard, and lemon zest and juice. Add olive oil and red wine vinegar. Taste and adjust seasoning. Dress the vegetables with the tarragon vinaigrette. Serve alongside the bruschetta.

½ cup tarragon, leaves picked and finely chopped

1 tablespoon Dijon mustard

Juice and zest of 1 lemon

3 tablespoons olive oil

3 tablespoons red wine vinegar

Grilled Butterflied Leg of Lamb with Mint Pesto

Serves: 8   Skill Level: **Moderate**   Prep Time: **30 minutes**   Cook Time: **30 to 45 minutes**
Inactive Cook Time: **2 hours to overnight**

We love this dish because it represents *The Chew* so perfectly. This leg of lamb is delicious, it's great for a celebration with friends and family, and the price is right. The mint pesto is a nice, fresh take on how to marry the flavors of lamb and mint without using the rather less inspired mint jelly of days past. Serve this with scallions and potatoes for the perfect meal at less than three dollars per person.

FOR THE LAMB:

1, 8-pound leg of lamb, deboned, excess fat trimmed, and butterflied

Salt and pepper

3 garlic cloves, peeled and cut into slices

2 sprigs fresh rosemary

½ cup extra-virgin olive oil

1 lemon

FOR THE MINT PESTO:

2 cups fresh mint leaves

1 cup basil

½ cup Parmigiano-Reggiano, freshly grated

½ cup pine nuts, toasted

2 garlic cloves

⅓ cup extra-virgin olive oil

Salt and pepper

TO MAKE THE LAMB:

1. Season the lamb with salt and pepper and then rub the garlic and rosemary all over the meat. Drizzle generously with olive oil and then place in a roasting pan to marinate. Cut the lemon in half and squeeze the juice over the lamb. Add the lemon to the pan. Marinate for a minimum of 2 hours, but preferably overnight.

2. Preheat a grill to medium-high heat. If using charcoal, allow your coals to burn until glowing with little visible flames. Remove the lamb from the refrigerator an hour before cooking to come to room temperature. Remove the lamb from the marinade, reserving marinade for basting.

3. Lay the lamb on the grill fat-side down. Cook for 15 to 20 minutes and flip to cook on the second side for 15 to 20 more minutes, basting with reserved marinade occasionally. Move the lamb to a cooler area on the grill if the meat starts to char too much. Remove from the grill when an instant-read thermometer registers 130°F for medium-rare. Allow to rest for 10 to 15 minutes before slicing. Reserve the juices from resting and pour over the sliced meat. Serve with the mint pesto.

TO MAKE THE MINT PESTO:

4. Combine all of the ingredients in a food processor, except the oil. Begin to puree while slowly adding the oil. Adjust seasoning to taste.

Braised Scallions and Potatoes

Serves: 8   Skill Level: **Easy**   Prep Time: **20 minutes**   Cook Time: **30 minutes**

This side dish is the perfect accompaniment to an Easter feast. Not only does it complement the traditional leg of lamb beautifully, but it is beautiful on its own. The light green of the scallions echoes new spring shoots coming up from the ground, promising warmer days and fresh blooms.

4 tablespoons butter, sliced

2 pounds tiny Yukon Gold potatoes, cut in half

1 garlic clove, cut into thick slices

2 bunches scallions, roots and greens trimmed; cut into 2-inch lengths

1 lemon, cut around the core into 4 pieces

Salt and freshly ground black pepper, to taste

1 cup Vin Santo or white wine

½ cup water

Extra-virgin olive oil, for drizzling

1. Place a heavy-bottomed pot over medium-high heat and add the butter. Toss in the potatoes, garlic, scallions, and lemon wedges and season generously with salt and pepper. Add the Vin Santo and water, bring to a simmer, and cover the pot with a lid.

2. Cook at a gentle simmer for 30 minutes, or until the potatoes are fork-tender. Taste and adjust seasoning. Serve with a drizzle of olive oil.

MARIO
Easter is *the* major religious holiday, which means it's the most sacred—and the most delicious.

Classic Carrot Cake with Whipped Cream Cheese Frosting

Serves: **8 to 10**   Skill Level: **Moderate**   Prep Time: **30 minutes**   Cook Time: **60 to 75 minutes**

The year was 1979. Jimmy Carter was in office, Suzanne Somers was making us laugh, and a young and already fabulous Clinton Kelly was spending his nights at home with his favorite dessert. Those long-gone Saturday nights, of listening to Olivia Newton-John and eating classic carrot cake with cream cheese frosting right out of the box, loom large in his memory. While Proust had a madeleine, Clinton has carrot cake. Take a whack at baking this classic and journey back to 1979 and Olivia belting out "Totally Hot."

FOR THE CAKE:

2 cups all-purpose flour

1 cup granulated sugar

½ cup brown sugar

2 teaspoons baking soda

1 teaspoon baking powder

1 teaspoon freshly grated cinnamon

1 teaspoon ground ginger

1 teaspoon allspice

½ teaspoon salt

2 cups grated carrots, packed

3 large eggs, whisked

¾ cup sour cream

½ cup vegetable oil

¾ cup walnuts, roughly chopped, plus more for garnish

¾ cup golden raisins, rehydrated in warm water for 10 minutes

TO MAKE THE CAKE:

1. Preheat oven to 350°F. In a large bowl, whisk together the flour, sugars, baking soda, baking powder, spices, and salt. Toss in the grated carrots and coat with flour, making sure the carrots aren't clumped together. Stir in the eggs, sour cream, and vegetable oil until a few streaks of dry mixture are still visible. Add the walnuts and raisins and fold in until the mixture is fully incorporated.

2. Pour into the prepared loaf pan and bake for 60 to 75 minutes, or until a skewer is inserted and comes out clean. Remove from oven and allow to cool completely on a wire rack.

TO MAKE THE FROSTING:

3. Whisk together the ingredients until the sugar is fully incorporated. Spread the frosting over the top of the cake and serve with walnuts to garnish.

FOR THE FROSTING:

12 ounces whipped cream cheese, at room temperature

4 tablespoons butter, softened

1 cup powdered sugar

1 teaspoon vanilla

Pinch of salt

Silk-Dyed Eggs

Making Easter eggs is one of the best parts of the holiday (next to doing an Easter egg hunt, eating chocolate from Easter baskets, hanging out with the Easter bunny . . . but I digress). Silk-dyed eggs are a way to get beautiful patterns and colors from old silk ties or scarves that aren't going to be worn again, but don't have to go to waste. The process for making these eggs is simple, but the results look like magic. Sort of like pulling a (Easter) rabbit out of a hat.

Eggs

100% silk scarves or ties

White cotton socks or other light-colored cotton cloth

Rubber bands

White vinegar

CLINTON
In France a bunny does not visit the children during Easter. Instead, a flying bell with wings zooms in from Rome and brings them chocolate and eggs on Easter morning.

1. Hard-boil or empty the eggs. To empty, poke a hole in the top and bottom of each egg and use a small straw to blow out the yolk and white. Rinse it out and let it dry. (Emptied eggs can be kept for much longer periods of time.)

2. If you are using ties, deconstruct them by snipping the stitching and removing the lining until you are left with only the silk. Cut the silk into pieces large enough to wrap around your eggs, plus a little extra to tie off.

3. Tightly wrap each egg in a scarf or tie with the silk flat against the egg's surface. Secure in place with a rubber band.

4. Wrap the covered egg in a sock or other cotton cloth and secure with a rubber band.

5. Add 1 cup of vinegar to a pot of gently boiling water. You want about 1 teaspoon of vinegar for every half cup of water. Be sure to use an enamel, glass, or other nonreactive pot.

6. Drop the eggs into the water and let sit at a gentle boil for 20 minutes. If they're blown eggs, fill them with water beforehand so they will sink.

7. Remove the eggs from the boiling water and allow them to cool completely.

8. Unwrap them and check out your creation!

MOTHER'S DAY

Perfect Mom-osa

Serves: **6 to 8**   Skill Level: **Easy**   Prep Time: **5 minutes**

Mimosas have become a staple of fancy breakfasts or brunches. And why not? The addition of fresh-squeezed OJ to sparkling wine is refreshing and delicious, plus the orange juice makes it feel a little breakfast-y. To get a fresh take on a mimosa, the trick is finding the right extra ingredient that will elevate the cocktail without robbing it of what makes it a classic. Elderflower liqueur does the trick. Elderflower liqueur is becoming more and more popular across the country and, of course, increasingly easier to find. With floral, honeyed, and fruity notes, elderflower liqueur adds depth, sophistication, and perfume to the mimosa. So let's call it the *mom*-osa for all those sophisticated ladies we love!

1 bottle prosecco or sparkling wine, chilled

4 ounces freshly squeezed orange juice, chilled

4 ounces elderflower liqueur, divided

Divide the orange juice and elderflower liqueur between each of the champagne flutes, and top with prosecco or sparkling wine. Enjoy!

DAPHNE

My mama always said, "Have standards, not expectations." Because for her, standards are things you hold for yourself and expectations are things that you put on other people, and you can't control other people so you set yourself up for disappointment. It's really cool and it actually works.

Daphne's mother, Lisa, receives flowers from her daughter on Mother's Day.

Frisée Salad with Candied Bacon

Serves: 4   Skill Level: **Moderate**   Prep Time: **20 minutes**   Cook Time: **25 to 30 minutes**

This is a classic French salad preparation but with an American touch that takes it over the top. Your mom may not have appreciated every moment you went over the top when you were growing up, but this time she'll approve. The French version includes the irresistible goodness of thick-cut, cubed bacon chunks, which are called *lardons*. Our version uses bacon, too, but the American kind, which has been gussied up with a mixture of sweetness and spice. Sugar and spice and everything nice—that was you when you were a teenager, right? *Wink!*

FOR THE VINAIGRETTE:

1 shallot, finely chopped

4 tablespoons champagne vinegar

3 tablespoons olive oil

Salt and freshly ground black pepper, to taste

FOR THE CANDIED BACON:

½ cup dark brown sugar

¼ cup maple syrup

⅛ teaspoon cayenne pepper (or more to taste)

1 tablespoon Dijon mustard

2 teaspoons apple cider vinegar

Salt and freshly ground black pepper

1 pound thick-cut bacon

FOR THE POACHED EGGS:

4 eggs

1 tablespoon vinegar

TO MAKE THE VINAIGRETTE:

1. Combine the shallot, vinegar, and oil in a small bowl. Season with salt and pepper and whisk. Set aside.

TO MAKE THE CANDIED BACON:

2. Preheat the oven to 350°F. Line a baking sheet with a silicone mat or foil and place a cooling rack on top. Stir together the dark brown sugar, maple syrup, cayenne pepper, Dijon mustard, and apple cider vinegar. Add freshly ground pepper, about 10 turns, and a pinch of salt. Add half the mixture to a baking dish and reserve the other half in a bowl.

3. Lay the bacon, piece by piece, in the baking dish, coating both sides, then transfer to the cooling rack. Lay the bacon in a single row on the rack. Place in the oven and let cook. After 15 minutes begin basting every 5 minutes until crispy, 25 to 30 minutes total. Remove from the oven and let cool on the rack for 5 minutes. Remove from the rack to prevent sticking and use, either whole or crumbled.

TO MAKE THE POACHED EGGS:

4. Bring a pot of water to a boil and add vinegar; reduce to a simmer. Working with one egg at a time, crack egg into water and cook 4 to 5 minutes. Remove with a slotted spoon.

TO MAKE THE SALAD:

FOR THE SALAD:

2 large heads frisée lettuce, bitter green leaves removed

Salt and freshly ground black pepper, to taste

Chives, for garnish

5. Cut the root end off the frisée and separate the leaves. Place in a large bowl and season with salt and pepper. Dress with the vinaigrette and toss.

6. Divide greens among four serving plates. Top each with a poached egg and candied bacon. Garnish with chives.

Bananas Foster Crepes

Serves: 6   Skill Level: **Moderate**   Prep Time: **20 minutes**   Cook Time: **30 to 45 minutes**

Inactive Prep Time: **10 minutes to 1 hour**

Traditional bananas Foster, which originated in New Orleans, is a terrific dessert. Topping vanilla ice cream with a mixture of bananas, butter, cinnamon, sugar, and rum, and then flambéing the whole thing . . . well, that's good stuff. But moms deserve the best, so we've taken bananas Foster and added the luxurious touch of buttery crepes to hold all that banana goodness. What was once only a dessert can now also be a sweet main dish at a decadent Mother's Day brunch.

FOR THE CREPES:

1½ cups all-purpose flour

4 eggs

2 cups whole milk

3 tablespoons extra-virgin olive oil

Pinch of salt

Butter, to oil crepe pan

FOR THE BANANAS FOSTER:

¼ cup butter

½ cup dark brown sugar

1 stick cinnamon

¼ teaspoon freshly grated nutmeg

2 teaspoons vanilla extract

4 bananas, diced

⅓ cup dark rum

FOR THE MELTED PEANUT BUTTER:

1 cup all-natural peanut butter

Water

Salt, to taste

Confectioners' sugar, to garnish

FOR THE CREPES:

1. Place the flour in a mixing bowl. Add the eggs one at a time, whisking to combine. Add the milk bit by bit and whisk to combine until all the milk is incorporated. Whisk in the extra-virgin olive oil. Season with salt and allow the batter to stand for 10 minutes to an hour.

2. Heat a 6-inch nonstick pan over high heat until hot and add a dab of butter. Turn the heat down to medium and pour 1½ tablespoons of batter into the pan and swirl to coat. Cook until pale golden on the bottom, about 1 minute. Flip and cook just 5 or 10 seconds on the second side. Remove and set aside. Continue the process until all the batter has been used. Keep warm on a plate and cover with a warm towel.

TO MAKE THE BANANAS FOSTER:

3. Melt the butter over medium heat in a large nonstick skillet. Add the brown sugar, spices, and vanilla and cook until caramelized, stirring occasionally. Toss in the bananas and coat with the sauce. Add the rum and flambé until flames extinguish.

TO MAKE THE MELTED PEANUT BUTTER:

4. Heat the peanut butter in a small saucepan over low, adding water as needed to thin to desired consistency. Season with salt to taste. Fill the crepes with a large spoonful of the filling and serve with a drizzle of melted peanut butter. Garnish with confectioners' sugar to serve.

Fruit Salad

Serves: 8   Skill Level: **Easy**   Prep Time: **30 minutes**

Fruit salad is only as good (and nutritious) as the fruit you put in it. Seems simple, right? But think of how many sad fruit salads you've been presented with over the years. Who thought that a few cubed apples and orange slices was an acceptable interpretation of what could be the star of any brunch? This fruit salad is spectacular because the fruit chosen for it is sweet, tart, soft, and toothsome, with vibrant colors that complement each other gorgeously. But a fruit salad without a little dressing is still, well, naked! In this case, we're using honey, lime juice, and thyme, with an optional splash of prosecco. If you and your guests think you aren't "fruit salad people," guess again!

3 freestone peaches, sliced and pits removed

3 plums, sliced and pits removed

3 nectarines, sliced and pits removed

1 pint blackberries

1 pint raspberries

Juice and zest of 2 limes

1 vanilla bean

2 tablespoons honey

2 sprigs of thyme, leaves only

1 tablespoon mint, leaves only and chopped

Whipped cream

1/2 bottle prosecco, optional

1. Combine all of the fruit in a large bowl. Squeeze lime juice over the fruit, then scrape vanilla bean into the bowl. Add lime zest, honey, and thyme to fruit. Fold everything together and allow the flavors to marry. Fold the mint into the whipped cream.

2. To serve, put fruit salad in a wine glass. Top each glass with whipped cream, and fill with prosecco if you'd like.

Michael cooks for his mom, Angel, in honor of Mother's Day.

Kid-Friendly Croissants

Serves: **4 to 6**   Skill Level: **Easy**   Cook Time: **25 to 30 minutes**

Croissants are a treat that we rarely think of making at home because making all that puff pastry is time-consuming and, if you're not a baker, hard to do! The solution, of course, lies in all the prepackaged puff pastry that's on the market. But if you use it to make plain croissants, they have the tendency to make you feel like you could do better. This recipe is the perfect compromise. The addition of sweet treats (in this case chocolate and almonds) makes for croissants that could have come from a French bakery. The beauty of these baked goodies is not only in the flavor but in the fact that they're so easy to make. The whole family can get involved, which is a lovely way to prepare for Mom's special day.

½ package frozen puff pastry, thawed

½ cup dark chocolate, chopped

½ cup almond paste

1 egg whisked with 2 tablespoons water

¼ cup sliced almonds

Confectioners' sugar, to dust

1. Preheat oven to 375°F. Line a baking sheet with parchment paper. Gently lay puff pastry out on flat surface. Cut into three equal rectangles. Cut each rectangle into two triangles by cutting diagonally lengthwise.

2. Place about a teaspoon of chocolate and almond paste in the center of the large end of the triangle pieces. Loosely roll toward the small end. Pinch the ends and bring them in to almost touch.

3. Place on the baking sheet, brush with the egg wash, and sprinkle with a few almond slices. Bake 25 to 30 minutes, or until the pastry is puffed and golden. Sprinkle with powdered sugar to serve.

DAPHNE

If you like these croissants, you will most likely fall in love with marzipan (particularly the chocolate-covered variety). If you haven't encountered it before, it's an almond-based candy that's so widely beloved, Iran, Germany, Italy, and Spain all claim to be the country of its origin. Once you take a bite, you won't care so much whence it hails so much as where you can get more.

Pressed Flower Cards

How many times have we heard our moms (and other loved ones) say that getting a homemade gift is wonderful because it's so personal and shows loving effort on the part of the gift giver? Let's just say, "A lot." Here's a way to make one-of-a-kind gift cards that are so beautiful they are gifts all on their own. This is another craft project that you can get the kids in on; it requires a delicate touch at the end, but getting them to choose the flowers and press them is tons of fun.

Dinner plates

Corrugated cardboard

Coffee filters

Paper

Flowers, preferably pansies or similar

Microwave

Paintbrush

Clear-drying craft glue

1. Turn a plate upside down, then cut cardboard to fit inside the rim of the plate. On top of that, stack 2 to 3 coffee filters and a piece of paper.

2. Snip the flower off of its stem and flatten nicely onto your paper. Then stack on top of the flower another piece of paper, 2 to 3 coffee filters, a piece of cardboard fitted to the rim of the plate, and a second plate, right side up.

3. Place stacked materials in the microwave for 40 seconds if drying just the blooms. (If you would like to dry the stems, it will take about a minute.)

4. Using clear glue, gently adhere the flower to a card. Be gentle, it's delicate! You may want to use tweezers to place your flowers. Cover with a thin coat of glue to seal and allow to dry.

Clinton embraces his number one fan—and mom—Terri.

MILESTONES

There are certain events in our lives that are cause for pull-out-all-the-stops celebrations. Why? Because they're about love: the love between two people who have decided to spend the rest of their lives together, love for a baby about to make his or her debut in the world, and love shared by a couple that has stood the test of time. Weddings, showers, and anniversaries are special occasions that are as varied as the people who celebrate them. But there's one thing that the most grandiose wedding and the most down-home baby shower have in common: food and drinks! Among the five of us, we've celebrated enough milestones to know what recipes will make the perfect menu for every gathering, whether it's your first or your fiftieth. So get ready to whip up some appetizers that will have your stodgy Aunt Margaret and your hippie cousin Sunshine bonding in no time!

SHOWER

Minted Watermelon and Cucumber Punch

Serves: **16**   Skill Level: **Easy**   Prep Time: **20 minutes**   Cook Time: **5 to 10 minutes**
Inactive Cook Time: **2 to 4 hours**

What's cooler than a cucumber? Cucumber ice cubes, of course! They are the X factor in this punch, which is so good that after one sip you'll be wondering where it's been all your life. The light and fresh flavors of cucumber and watermelon mingle with mint simple syrup for a sweet, crisp taste that just hits the spot. So make up a big batch for your wedding or baby shower. Even the mom-to-be can have a glass, because it's non-alcoholic!

FOR THE SIMPLE SYRUP:

½ bunch fresh mint leaves, plus more for garnish

½ cup sugar

½ cup water

FOR THE PUNCH:

2 English cucumbers, peeled and cubed, plus more cucumber slices for garnish

2 cups cubed watermelon

¼ cup lime juice

24 ounces club soda

TO MAKE THE SIMPLE SYRUP:

1. Place mint leaves in a heatproof bowl. In a medium saucepot, stir together the sugar and water over medium-high heat. Once the sugar has dissolved, remove from heat and pour into the heatproof bowl with the mint leaves. Allow to steep until cooled to room temperature. Strain out the mint leaves. Simple syrup can be made a week ahead and stored in the fridge.

TO MAKE THE PUNCH:

2. Place half of the cucumber cubes on a sheet tray and freeze for 2 hours.

3. Place the watermelon in a food processor and puree. Strain through a mesh sieve to remove pulp and seeds. Repeat the process with the remaining cucumber cubes.

4. Stir together the watermelon and cucumber juices. Add the minted simple syrup and lime juice. Chill mixture until ready to serve. Place a few cubes of frozen cucumber into each glass. Fill each glass two-thirds full with the punch. Top off with club soda and garnish with mint sprigs and sliced cucumber.

Sausage and Swiss Chard Frittata

Serves: 6 to 8   Skill Level: Easy   Prep Time: 10 minutes   Cook Time: 20 to 25 minutes

Celebrating, whether it's for an upcoming wedding or a baby on the way, can work up quite the appetite. That's why you need a filling, crowd-pleasing source of sustenance to serve your shower guests. Sausage, egg, and cheese are a no-fail breakfast combination. But add some crunchy greens and you're really in business. The terrific texture of Swiss chard is what takes this frittata to the next level, so the key is not to cook it down too much. Keep that healthy crunch in the game! Throw in some onions and top it off with the delicious, salty, lactic love that is Pecorino Romano cheese and you've got a solid spin on a breakfast classic.

2 tablespoons extra-virgin olive oil

1 pound spicy Italian sausage, removed from casing

1 red onion, thinly sliced

2 bunches Swiss chard, chiffonade, thinly sliced

3 cloves garlic, minced

8 eggs

Salt and freshly ground black pepper, to taste

½ cup freshly grated Pecorino

1. Preheat oven to 350°F. In a large nonstick, ovenproof pan over medium-high heat, add the olive oil. Add the sausage, and cook until crisp, about 8 minutes, breaking it up as it cooks. Add the red onion and chard, then cook 2 more minutes. Crack the eggs into a large bowl, add the garlic, and whisk together. Transfer sauté pan contents to bowl with the egg mixture, and stir to mix everything. Season generously with salt and pepper.

2. Transfer back to ovenproof pan and stir with a spatula to make sure it doesn't stick. Place in the oven and cook until set, about 15 minutes. Then sprinkle with Pecorino and cool for about 5 minutes before serving.

MARIO
I crave salty, spicy stuff. I'll get a raw jalapeño out of the fridge, smear a little cream cheese on it, then sprinkle it with kosher salt and, on top of that, add chipotle Tabasco sauce. That scratches my itch.

Baby Cucumber Sandwiches

Serves: 8 to 10   Skill Level: Easy   Prep Time: 20 minutes

When you're celebrating a baby on the way, you've gotta think "adorable." These dainty cucumber sandwiches totally fit the bill! A blend of goat cheese, cream cheese, and butter complements that cool cucumber crunch to perfection. The best thing about this classic appetizer is it brings a casual elegance to the table for an incredibly low cost. Of course, there's also the fact that these are just about the easiest things you can whip up for a party. I mean, come on. You can handle a sandwich, right?

8 ounces goat cheese, room temperature

4 ounces cream cheese, room temperature

4 tablespoons unsalted butter, room temperature

1 garlic clove, minced

3 tablespoons grated Parmesan

3 tablespoons fresh dill, minced

1 tablespoon parsley, minced

Pinch salt

¼ teaspoon freshly ground black pepper

10 slices pumpernickel bread

6 Persian cucumbers (washed and thinly sliced)

1. In a standing mixer, mix the goat cheese, cream cheese, butter, and minced garlic. Add the Parmesan, dill, parsley, salt, and pepper; combine well. Pack the mixture into an airtight container, and store in the refrigerator. To serve, bring to room temperature before spreading on sandwiches.

2. Place the thinly sliced cucumbers on a clean kitchen towel or paper towel to remove excess moisture. Smear a layer of goat cheese spread on one side of each piece of bread. Shingle the cucumbers over half of the slices. Top with remaining slices of bread, cheese-side down. Trim the crust from the sandwiches and cut each sandwich into four pieces. Serve chilled or at room temperature.

CARLA
I think women's cravings are different from men's cravings. Men may think, "Oh, I kind of want that." Women crave it. We want it. We need it.

Baby Chicken Salad Puffs

Serves: 8 to 10   Skill Level: **Moderate**   Prep Time: **15 minutes**   Cook Time: **35 to 40 minutes**

No wedding shower or baby shower (well, any shower, really) is complete without teeny, tiny little hors d'oeuvres. Canapés and snacks come in all shapes and sizes, but this one is a winner on several levels. These baby chicken salad puffs taste great, are an economical choice, and are easy to assemble. All it takes is a little cream puff shell to turn a basic mayonnaise-based salad into a fancy, beautiful treat that's way simpler to make than it looks. They're not just for showers, either: whip them up anytime you're entertaining at lunch and watch your guests flip over your Pinterest-worthy party skills!

FOR THE PUFFS:

1 cup water

5 tablespoons butter, cubed

1 teaspoon sugar

½ teaspoon salt

1 cup all-purpose flour

6 large eggs, plus 1 yolk

2 tablespoons water

FOR THE CHICKEN SALAD:

1 cup mayonnaise

Juice and zest of 1 lemon

3 tablespoons fresh tarragon, chopped

⅓ cup walnuts, toasted and chopped

⅓ cup raisins

3 cups store-bought rotisserie chicken, diced

TO MAKE THE PUFFS:

1. Preheat oven to 400°F. Line two baking sheets with parchment paper or silicone mats.

2. In a medium saucepot over medium-high heat, combine the water, butter, sugar, and salt and bring to a simmer. Once the butter has melted, whisk in flour, breaking up any lumps. Once the dough forms a ball and pulls away from the pan, remove from heat. Beat in one egg at a time, fully incorporating after each addition. The dough will be glossy and thick.

3. If using parchment, lift the corners of the parchment. Place a small amount of the batter onto the baking sheet, then press parchment back in place. This will prevent the parchment from slipping.

4. Using two spoons, place small balls of the batter (about 1 inch), spacing 1 to 2 inches apart, in rows on each baking sheet. Dampen your finger with water to smooth out the shape of the tops as needed. In a small bowl, whisk together the remaining egg yolk and water. Using a pastry brush, brush the top of each puff with the egg wash. Bake for 20 minutes or until puffed, glossy, and rich gold on the outside.

5. Remove from oven and allow to cool completely. The puffs can be made a few days in advance and stored in an airtight container at room temperature.

TO MAKE THE CHICKEN SALAD:

6. Stir together the ingredients in a large bowl and allow to chill until ready to use. This can be prepared a day in advance and stored in a covered container in the fridge.

7. Slice each puff in half along the equator. Place a scoop of chicken salad on each bottom piece. Return the other half to top off sandwiches. Serve at room temperature.

Chocolate Truffles

Serves: **30**   Skill Level: **Easy**   Prep Time: **25 minutes**   Cook Time: **5 to 10 minutes**

Inactive Cook Time: **2 to 6 hours**

As you know, I'm a meat guy. Sweets aren't really my thing. But even I love to have a little fun with chocolate, and I'm not gonna argue with a classic truffle. The great thing about these little balls of gourmet goodness is that you can roll them in whatever ingredient your heart desires. Sprinkles? Coconut? Bacon? Wasabi? It's all up to you. You can use pink and blue sprinkles for a baby shower, or black and white sprinkles for a wedding shower. The best part is you're taking a gourmet sweet that costs a fortune at the store and whipping it up for pennies on the dollar. Talk about sweetening the deal.

8 ounces semisweet or bittersweet chocolate, cut into small pieces

½ cup heavy whipping cream

2 tablespoons unsalted butter, cut into small pieces

2 tablespoons rum or bourbon, optional

Bacon

Chili powder

Coconut

Hazelnut, crushed

Crystallized ginger

Wasabi powder

Pop Rocks

Sea salt

Lime zest

Unsweetened cocoa powder

Heath bar, crushed

Peppermint candies, crushed

Pretzels, crushed

Sprinkles

1. Place the chopped chocolate in a medium-sized heatproof bowl. Set aside.

2. Heat the cream and butter in a small saucepan over medium heat. Bring just to a boil. Immediately pour the boiling cream over the chocolate and allow to stand for a minute or two. Stir with a rubber spatula until smooth. (If the chocolate doesn't melt completely, place in the microwave for about 20 seconds, or over a saucepan of simmering water, just until melted.) If desired, add the liquor.

3. Cover and place in the refrigerator until the chocolate mixture is firm. This will take several hours.

4. Place your coatings for the truffles on a plate. Remove the truffle mixture from the refrigerator. With your hands or a small melon baller, form the chocolate into round or misshaped bite-sized balls. Immediately roll the truffle in the coating and place on a parchment-lined baking sheet or tray.

5. Cover and place in the refrigerator until firm, about an hour. The truffles can be refrigerated for a couple of weeks or else frozen for a couple of months. Bring to room temperature before serving.

Banana Bread Pudding

Serves: **10**   Skill Level: **Easy**   Prep Time: **20 minutes**   Cook Time: **1 hour, 10 minutes**

Bananas and croissants are brunch basics, but put them together in a pudding and your shower guests are going to go gaga! A creamy custard is the base of this decadent dish, but it's the croissants that really transform the concept of bread pudding into something that'll blow your mind. While you're at it, don't hold back with the nutmeg and vanilla. This recipe is all about finding your own balance of savory and sweet, and you really can't go wrong. The proof is in the pudding. Isn't that how it goes?

FOR THE BANANA BREAD PUDDING:

1 tablespoon butter, softened

3 large eggs

3 large egg yolks

2½ cups half-and-half

2 cups whole milk

1 cup sugar

1½ teaspoons vanilla

Pinch salt

½ teaspoon freshly grated nutmeg

6 croissants, preferably day old, sliced in half

2 cups sliced bananas

FOR THE CHOCOLATE SAUCE:

1 cup heavy cream

¼ cup sugar

Pinch salt

4 ounces semisweet chocolate, chopped

1 tablespoon unsweetened cocoa powder

TO MAKE THE PUDDING:

1. Preheat oven to 350°F. Grease a 9- x 13-inch pan with the softened butter, and set aside. Whisk together the eggs, yolks, half-and-half, milk, sugar, vanilla, salt, and nutmeg.

2. Place the bottom halves of the croissants in the prepared pan. Add the bananas in an even layer, and then add the top halves of the croissants. Pour the custard over the top, then press down slightly and let soak for at least 10 minutes.

3. Cover the pan with foil, tented with a few holes poked through, and bake for 45 minutes. Uncover, then bake for another 20 minutes until the pudding puffs and the custard is set. Remove from the oven to cool slightly while you prepare the chocolate sauce.

TO MAKE THE CHOCOLATE SAUCE:

4. Place the cream, sugar, and salt in a medium saucepot over medium heat. Bring the cream to a simmer and stir until the sugar dissolves. When the sugar has dissolved, add the chocolate and cocoa powder, whisking until they have melted and everything is combined.

5. Drizzle over the banana bread pudding to serve.

MICHAEL
My mom is four feet eleven, and was eighty-five pounds before she got pregnant with me. I was a nine-pound baby. I was a tenth of her weight at birth.

Citrus Salt Scrub

When you throw a shower, you want to send your guests home with a favor that will have them oohing and aahing long after the party is over. This citrus salt scrub fits the bill perfectly! The zesty fragrance wakes up the senses while the simple, all-natural ingredients will leave you feeling scrubbed, polished, and ready to face the day. All you need is some salt, coconut oil, and the zest of your favorite citrus fruit. And don't think you have to choose just one! Try a lemon-lime blend or throw them all into the mix for the ultimate aromatic pick-me-up.

½ cup coconut oil (or almond, olive, or vegetable oil)

½ cup sea salt

1½ teaspoons citrus zest (lemon, lime, orange, grapefruit, or a combination)

TO MAKE THE SCRUB:

1. Place coconut oil in a large bowl and microwave at intervals of 10 seconds until completely melted. (If using almond, olive, or vegetable oil, it will already be liquid.) Once the oil is liquid, add sea salt and citrus zest. Make sure to not allow any water near the bowl as water will dissolve the salt.

2. Pour mixture into airtight containers. Decorate with names or notes for guests.

3. Store in a cool, dry place.

TO USE THE SCRUB:

While in the shower, mix the ingredients with your fingertips. Apply the body scrub with hands or soft washcloth. Rinse the mixture off completely.

WEDDING

Love Drunk Punch

Serves: **8 to 10**   Skill Level: **Easy**   Prep Time: **10 minutes**   Cook Time: **20 minutes**

Many weddings will offer a full bar where guests can procure their usual libation. But why not offer them something unique that sets your party apart from the rest? This time around, we're not going for your typical fizzy, fruity refreshment. The unexpected depth of this drink comes from mixing orange and lemon with the warming winter flavors of mulled cider. For an impressive touch, stud some oranges and lemons with cloves and toss them in the bowl. Wait, am I forgetting something? Oh yeah: BOURBON. Just kidding. I never forget that part. Fill 'er up!

½ gallon apple cider

1 tablespoon mulling spices

Peel of 1 orange

½ cup orange juice

1 tablespoon lemon juice

1 cup bourbon or Calvados

1 bottle sparkling wine

Lemon and orange slices, for garnish

Whole cloves, for garnish

1. Combine the cider, mulling spices, and orange peel in a medium pot and cook on low heat for 20 minutes. Strain and let cool.

2. Add the orange juice, lemon juice, bourbon, and sparkling wine. Garnish with lemon and orange slices studded with cloves.

Ham Croquettes

Serves: **30**   Skill Level: **Moderate**   Prep Time: **30 minutes**   Cook Time: **35 to 40 minutes**
Inactive Cook Time: **2 hours**

When you have guests coming from many different places, backgrounds, and walks of life, there's just nothing that will bring them together like a good old-fashioned comfort food. Ham croquettes are crunchy on the outside, creamy on the inside, and full of classic, dependable flavors that warm your heart up right along with your stomach. It's cheesy, but hey, so are these croquettes. Serve them during the cocktail hour of your wedding celebration and watch the bride's shy aunt and the groom's crazy uncle bond over their common love of good food.

4 tablespoons unsalted butter

¼ cup olive oil

¾ cup flour, plus more for breading

4 cups whole milk

2½ teaspoons salt, plus more to taste

1 teaspoon freshly grated nutmeg

Freshly ground black pepper, to taste

1 cup Manchego cheese, finely shredded

1 cup cooked ham, finely chopped

Oil for frying (vegetable or peanut)

6 eggs, beaten

2 cups panko bread crumbs

1. Place a heavy-bottomed enameled pot over medium heat. When the pot is hot, add the butter and olive oil. Cook, stirring occasionally, for 2 to 3 minutes. Next, whisk in ¾ cup flour. When all of the flour has absorbed, slowly whisk in 1 cup of the milk. Whisk until no more lumps appear, then whisk in the rest of the milk. Season with salt, nutmeg, and pepper. Bring the milk to a gentle boil while whisking, then reduce the heat to low. Cook, stirring frequently, for 30 minutes. Next mix in the cheese and stir until completely melted. Mix in the ham, then pour the mix into a 9- x 13-inch pan and chill thoroughly, about 2 hours.

2. Fill a large Dutch oven halfway up with oil and heat oil to 360°F. While the oil is heating, form your croquettes. Using a 1-tablespoon measuring spoon, scoop out the chilled mixture into balls. With floured hands, roll them, and then place on a baking sheet or plate while you finish the rest. They can be kept in the refrigerator at this point until ready to bread and fry.

3. Set up a breading station with flour, eggs, and bread crumbs in separate shallow dishes. Dredge the balls in the flour, then the beaten egg, and then the bread crumbs, shaking off any excess. Drop into the heated oil and fry for 1 to 2 minutes per side, moving them around until completely golden brown. Remove from the oil with a slotted spoon to a paper towel–lined plate and season lightly with salt. Cool for a few minutes before serving.

Tuna Tartare

Serves: 12   Skill Level: **Moderate**   Prep Time: **30 minutes**   Cook Time: **12 to 15 minutes**

After a wedding ceremony is over, guests are sure to be hankering for a bite to eat. So it's important to have light-yet-satisfying appetizers awaiting them at the reception. This recipe easily meets those criteria, plus it's a bit more exotic than the typical chips and dip. But when it comes to tuna tartare, there's no messing around: get thee to the fish store and grab a piece of sushi-grade tuna. Then get ready to utilize some of the best flavors of Japanese cuisine with a little bit of ginger, a little bit of sesame, and, of course, a kick of wasabi. It's all about freshness with this dish, so hold off on mixing everything together until your guests have their wonton chips poised. Ready, set, dip!

FOR THE TUNA TARTARE:

1 pound sushi-quality tuna, small dice

1 avocado, diced

⅛ cup canola oil

½ teaspoon peeled and finely grated ginger

1 teaspoon finely chopped jalapeño

1 teaspoon wasabi powder

1 scallion, green and white parts, finely diced

Salt and freshly ground black pepper, to taste

Wonton chips, to serve

FOR THE WONTON CHIPS:

18 square wonton wrappers

Vegetable oil spray or melted butter

Sea salt

½ teaspoon black sesame seeds

½ teaspoon white sesame seeds

TO MAKE THE TUNA TARTARE:

1. Place the diced tuna into a bowl and place that bowl over an additional bowl filled with ice to keep the tuna cold. Cover the tuna with plastic and keep in the fridge until ready to serve.

2. In a separate bowl, combine the avocado, oil, ginger, jalapeño, wasabi powder, and scallion. Season with salt and pepper and fold in the chilled tuna.

TO MAKE THE WONTON CHIPS:

3. Preheat oven to 350°F. Cut the wonton wrappers in half diagonally, and arrange them on a cookie sheet.

4. Spray with vegetable oil or brush lightly with melted butter. Top with sea salt and sesame seeds.

5. Bake for 12 to 15 minutes until golden brown and crisp. Allow the chips to come to room temperature.

6. Arrange the wonton chips on a platter and place a heaping tablespoon of the tuna mixture in the center of each chip. Serve immediately.

Striped Bass in Cartoccio

Serves: 4   Skill Level: **Easy**   Prep Time: **20 minutes**   Cook Time: **12 to 14 minutes**

When people receive wedding invitations, they are sometimes asked to choose an entrée on their RSVP cards. Check one: beef, chicken, or fish. Well, this striped bass will have everyone wishing they had checked the fish box! *Cartoccio* is just the name for the simple technique of baking things in parchment paper. It holds your fish and vegetables together and steams them at the same time. Better yet, it gives the dish a beautiful presentation that's as inexpensive as it is impressive. If sea bass isn't your thing, no problem. Go to your local fishmonger or seafood market and pick up whatever fish you like.

4, 6-ounce fillets of wild striped bass

Salt and freshly ground black pepper, to taste

1 small yellow squash, julienned

2 carrots, peeled and julienned

1 bulb fresh fennel, julienned

10 leaves Swiss chard, trimmed and chiffonade

4 branches fresh oregano

1 bunch Italian parsley, chopped to ¼ cup yield

12 Gaeta olives

1 cup white wine

¼ cup extra-virgin olive oil

1. Preheat the oven to 450°F. Cut four pieces of parchment into 12-inch squares. Season each piece of fish with salt and pepper. Mix the vegetables in a bowl and season with salt and pepper. Divide the mixed vegetables evenly among the centers of the four pieces of paper.

2. Place 1 fish fillet over the vegetables and 1 branch of oregano over the fillet. Divide the parsley, olives, and wine evenly over the fish fillets and add a generous drizzle of olive oil. Fold up each packet and seal the edges by folding them over several times.

3. Bake in the oven for 12 to 14 minutes, and serve hot. Watch out for the steam that will blast from the hot packet once opened.

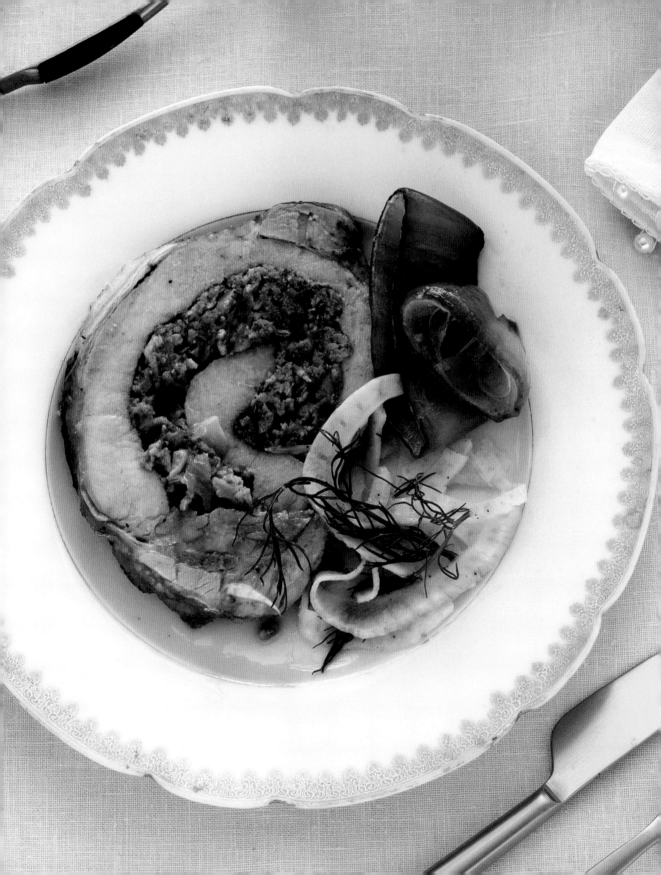

Arista alla Porchetta

Serves: **16**   Skill Level: **Moderate**   Prep Time: **30 minutes**   Cook Time: **1 hour, 25 minutes**

No one speaks the language of love quite like the Italians do. So I'm about to show you one of my favorite celebratory dishes. It's hearty, it's delicious, and it has the added bonus of the fact that you can serve it up at room temperature. *Arista alla porchetta* is perfect for a main course not only at a wedding, but at a quiet dinner with a loved one as well. After all, *arista* means "the very best" in the Tuscan dialect!

1, 4-pound boneless pork loin roast, butterflied

Salt and freshly ground black pepper

½ cup extra-virgin olive oil

1 medium onion, thinly sliced

1 fennel bulb, trimmed, fronds reserved and chopped, bulb thinly sliced

2 pounds ground pork shoulder

2 tablespoons fennel seeds

2 tablespoons chopped fresh rosemary

6 cloves garlic, thinly sliced

1 cup fresh bread crumbs

2 large eggs, lightly beaten

4 red onions, cut in half

1 lemon, halved

1. Lay the pork loin flat and sprinkle with salt and pepper. Set aside. In a 10- to 12-inch sauté pan, heat ¼ cup of the olive oil over medium-high heat until it begins to smoke. Add the sliced onion and fennel bulb and sauté until softened and lightly browned, about 10 minutes. Add the ground pork, fennel seeds, rosemary, garlic, and 2 tablespoons pepper, and cook, stirring occasionally, until the pork is no longer pink, about 10 minutes. Transfer to a bowl and allow to cool. Preheat the oven to 425°F.

2. Add all but 1 tablespoon of the fennel fronds, the bread crumbs, and eggs to the pork mixture and mix gently. Spread the mixture over the pork loin. Roll it up, starting from a long side, like a jelly roll, and tie with butcher's twine. Place the red onions in a roasting pan and set the pork on top. Roast for 1 hour and 15 minutes, or until the internal temperature is 135°F. Remove and let rest for 10 minutes.

3. Slice the pork into one-inch-thick pieces. Serve drizzled with the remaining ¼ cup olive oil and a good squeeze of lemon, garnished with the reserved fennel fronds, and with the onions on the side.

MARIO
You may not think that garlic would be right for a romantic wedding dinner, but as long as you eat the same amount of garlic as the person that you're going to kiss, you'll be fine.

Cheese Tart with Marinated Tomato Zucchini Salad

Serves: **8**   Skill Level: **Easy**   Prep Time: **25 minutes**   Cook Time: **30 to 35 minutes**
Inactive Cook Time: **1 hour**

When serving appetizers at a wedding, it's good to have some stationary items that guests can devour at will, and also to have some food passed butler-style. This baked tart, which combines a savory crust, a cheesy filling, and a super-simple tomato zucchini salad, can be cut up into bite-sized pieces and doled out to guests. Be sure to make enough, because your friends and family will flock to the servers who pass out this amazing hors d'oeuvre!

FOR THE TOMATO ZUCCHINI SALAD:

1 cup cherry tomatoes, cut in half

½ cup zucchini, sliced along full length into thin strips

½ teaspoon red chili flakes

1 garlic clove, smashed

3 tablespoons red wine vinegar

2 tablespoons olive oil

Salt and freshly ground black pepper, to taste

¼ cup basil leaves, torn

FOR THE TART:

1 sheet puff pastry, thawed

2 tablespoons butter, melted

1 egg, beaten

½ cup ricotta, room temperature

½ cup goat cheese, room temperature

¼ cup Parmesan, grated

TO MAKE THE TOMATO ZUCCHINI SALAD:

1. Combine the tomatoes, zucchini, chili flakes, smashed garlic, red wine vinegar, and olive oil in a medium-sized bowl. Season with salt and pepper and then set aside to marinate at room temperature for 1 hour.

TO MAKE THE TART:

2. Preheat the oven to 350°F. Lay the puff pastry on a parchment-lined baking sheet. With a paring knife, lightly trace a 1-inch border around the puff pastry; then, with a fork, dock (or poke holes) all over the inside rectangle. Brush the edges of the puff pastry with melted butter. Place in the oven and cook for 10 minutes. The edges that were not docked should puff up and create a free-form tart shell. Remove from the oven and let cool slightly.

3. In a medium bowl, combine the egg, ricotta, goat cheese, Parmesan, lemon zest, and herbs. Season with salt and pepper and stir to combine evenly. Taste and adjust seasoning if necessary. Spoon the cheese mixture into the center of the tart and smear with a spatula to fill in the edges. Bake the tart for 15 to 20 minutes, or until the cheese is melted and the tart is golden. Remove from the oven and let cool.

Zest of 1 lemon

1 tablespoon chives, finely chopped

1 tablespoon tarragon, leaves finely chopped

1 tablespoon parsley, finely chopped

Salt and freshly ground black pepper, to taste

4. Right before serving, remove the garlic from the tomato mixture. Strain the mixture and then toss with the basil leaves. Reseason with salt and pepper. Top the cheese tart with the tomato zucchini salad, cut into pieces, and serve.

Mini Baked Alaska

Serves: **12**   Skill Level: **Difficult**   Prep Time: **30 minutes**   Cook Time: **15 to 20 minutes**
Inactive Prep Time: **30 minutes to 1 hour**

At most weddings, the dessert option is a foregone conclusion: wedding cake. But it doesn't have to be that way! Other sweets can be served in place of, or in addition to, the cake. Because let's be honest: you can never have too much dessert! Baked Alaska is a five-star dessert that proves looking fancy doesn't have to be expensive. We're making our version small and cute, and there's something about taking our largest state and making it itty-bitty that tickles me. But make sure you've got your timing right: these babies have to be fired up just moments before serving or the little Alaskas will begin to melt!

FOR THE PECAN SHORTBREAD COOKIES:

1 cup flour

¼ cup sugar

¼ teaspoon salt

1 tablespoon toasted pecans, very finely ground

½ cup unsalted butter, chilled

¾ teaspoon vanilla

TO ASSEMBLE:

1 pint chocolate sorbet

¼ cup orange liqueur

FOR THE MERINGUE:

8 egg whites

⅛ teaspoon salt

½ teaspoon cream of tartar

2 cups superfine sugar

1 teaspoon vanilla

1 tablespoon orange zest

TO MAKE THE PECAN SHORTBREAD COOKIES:

1. Whisk the flour, sugar, salt, and ground pecans in a medium bowl to blend. Add butter and vanilla. Crumble together with fingers until the dough resembles peas. Form the dough into a disk and chill for 10 minutes.

2. Preheat oven to 350°F. Roll out dough to about ¼-inch thickness. Cut out cookies using a 2-inch circular cookie cutter. Place on a baking sheet about 1 inch apart. Bake for 15 to 20 minutes until pale gold. Allow to cool.

TO ASSEMBLE:

3. Using a 4-ounce ice cream scoop, scoop chocolate sorbet onto each of the cookies. Transfer to the freezer so that the sorbet hardens.

TO MAKE THE MERINGUE:

4. Using an electric mixer fitted with whisk attachment, beat the egg whites and salt on low speed until foamy. Add the cream of tartar and beat on medium speed until soft peaks form. Beating constantly, add the superfine sugar in a slow, steady stream. Add the vanilla and zest and beat on high speed until the egg whites are very stiff. Scrape into a pastry bag and immediately pipe the meringue, starting at the

base of the sorbet, in a circle around the cookie. Continue to pipe in a spiral pattern until you reach the top.

5. Sprinkle a few drops of orange liqueur onto each dollop of meringue and then light the alcohol on fire. It will cook the meringue just enough, while not melting the sorbet. Serve immediately.

Lemon Cardamom Cookie Wedding Gifts

Serves: 96   **Skill Level:** Easy   **Prep Time:** 45 minutes   **Cook Time:** 18 to 20 minutes   **Inactive Prep Time:** 12 hours

Lots of couples like to give out personalized favors at their weddings. They can range from coasters to magnets to candles. But wouldn't you rather give your guests something they can eat?! That's right, I'm about to switch things up a bit with the perfect bite-sized treat that all your guests will love. And you'll love them even more: not only are these shortbread cookies hard to mess up, but you can make them ahead of time and save yourself a load of stress before the big day. These cookies are delicious and delightful, and they'll save you the expense of engraving picture frames or wine glasses. What more could you ask for?

FOR THE LEMON SUGAR:

Zest of 3 lemons

2 cups powdered sugar

FOR THE COOKIES:

1 pound unsalted butter, room temperature

1 cup powdered sugar

1 tablespoon vanilla extract

2 teaspoons lemon juice

2 teaspoons lemon zest

2 teaspoons orange zest

1½ teaspoons salt

1½ cups pistachios, ground; or 1 cup walnuts, ground

4½ cups all-purpose flour

2 teaspoons ground cardamom

TO MAKE THE LEMON SUGAR:

1. Line a baking sheet with waxed paper. Spread the lemon zest onto the prepared baking sheet trying to avoid clumps. Place the baking sheet in a cold oven and allow to sit overnight. The zest should be dry before combining with the sugar.

2. Pulse the zest and sugar together in a food processor until evenly distributed. Set aside until ready to roll the cookies.

TO MAKE THE COOKIES:

3. Preheat oven to 350°F. Line baking sheets with parchment paper. Using an electric mixer, beat together the butter and sugar until fluffy. Add the vanilla, lemon juice, zests, and salt and beat until combined. In a medium bowl, whisk together the flour, ground nuts, and cardamom until combined. Add the flour to the butter mixture in three additions, mixing after each, and making sure not to overmix the dough.

4. Using a tablespoon or 1-ounce ice cream scoop, portion out dough and roll into balls. Place the cookies about 1½ inches apart on the prepared baking sheets. Bake for 18 to 20 minutes trying to avoid brown spots but making sure the top is just firm to the touch.

5. Meanwhile, place the lemon sugar in a rimmed baking dish or pie plate. Remove the cookies from the oven and allow to cool slightly. The cookies should still be warm when rolling in the lemon sugar. Roll the cookies to coat completely in the flavored sugar and allow to cool completely on a wire rack. Reserve the remaining lemon sugar.

6. These cookies can be baked up to one month in advance and stored in the freezer in an airtight container. When ready to serve or package, roll them again in the lemon sugar to heavily coat.

7. Place several cookies in a small tin or other type of container. Tie ribbon with names or notes for your guests.

ANNIVERSARY PARTY

Strawberry-Sage Lemonade

Serves: **1**   Skill Level: **Easy**   Prep Time: **10 minutes**   Cook Time: **20 minutes**
Inactive Prep Time: **1 hour**

What does a great marriage have in common with this drink? Lots! You take some amazing yet different ingredients that easily stand on their own, and you mix them up to create a whole new experience! "Strawberries and sage?" you might ask. "Would you really put those things together?" Well, why not? Just look at ham and pineapple . . . peanut butter and bacon . . . potato chips and chocolate. Sometimes you just need to push the envelope to discover new recipes for success. That goes for your cocktails and your marriage.

FOR THE STRAWBERRY-SAGE PUREE:

1 quart strawberries, rinsed and tops removed

8 sage leaves

1 tablespoon sugar

FOR THE COCKTAIL:

Juice of half a lemon

1 ounce strawberry-sage puree

1½ ounces vodka

Seltzer, to top off drink

Lemon slices, for garnish

TO MAKE THE STRAWBERRY-SAGE PUREE:

1. Preheat oven to 425°F. Toss the strawberries and sage leaves in the sugar. Spread on a sheet tray and roast for 20 minutes. Allow to cool slightly, and then puree in a food processor. Chill in the refrigerator for at least an hour.

TO MAKE THE COCKTAIL:

2. In a highball glass, combine the lemon juice, strawberry-sage puree, and vodka and stir to combine. Top with seltzer and garnish with a lemon slice.

Spinach Artichoke Dip

Serves: **8**   Skill Level: **Easy**   Prep Time: **15 minutes**   Cook Time: **20 minutes**

Whether it's your fifth or your fiftieth, your anniversary deserves to be celebrated with some mouthwatering food. And I think it's written somewhere that no celebration is complete without a really delectable dip. Here's one that's oh, so delicious, your guests will be fighting for the last scoop. Plus, it's got spinach and artichokes. That's healthy stuff!

⅓ cup mayonnaise

⅓ cup cream cheese

¼ cup sour cream

1 cup freshly grated Parmesan

1 cup chopped marinated artichokes, drained and rinsed

2 cups chopped frozen spinach, thawed and drained

2 tablespoons roasted garlic

Salt and freshly ground black pepper, to taste

Tortilla chips, to serve

1. Preheat oven to 375°F. In a large mixing bowl, stir together all ingredients and season to taste. Transfer to a 4-cup ramekin. Bake for 20 minutes or until bubbling and slightly golden on top.

2. Serve warm with tortilla chips.

CLINTON
If you are cooking for a large crowd, you can make this in two, 2-cup ramekins. Keep one warm in the oven while your guests eat the other and you'll always have hot dip.

Orecchiette with Romano Beans

Serves: **6**   Skill Level: **Moderate**   Prep Time: **1 hour**   Cook Time: **10 minutes**

Say *buongiorno* to another one of my favorite classic Italian meals, orecchiette with Romano beans. This wonderful pasta dish hails from the Puglia region of southern Italy, where the olive oil– and vegetable-based culture produces some of my favorite foods in the world. The sauce calls for Romano beans, but if you can't find those, any waxy green bean will do. In fact, the dish is all about making do with what you have, which is why there are no eggs in the dough.

FOR THE ORECCHIETTE:

2 cups semolina flour

2 cups all-purpose flour

1–1¼ cups tepid water

FOR THE SAUCE:

4 tablespoons extra-virgin olive oil

1 pound Romano beans, ends removed, and cut into ½-inch pieces

½ stalk celery, thinly sliced

2 serrano chilies, thinly sliced

1 onion, cut into ½-inch dice

Salt, to taste

1 teaspoon red pepper flakes

½ cup freshly grated caciocavallo cheese (plus more for garnish)

TO MAKE THE ORECCHIETTE:

1. Combine both flours in a mound in the center of a large wooden cutting board. Make a well in the center of the flour and add water a little at a time, stirring with your hands until dough is formed. As you incorporate the water, keep pushing the flour up to retain the well shape (do not worry if it looks messy). The dough will come together when about half of the flour is incorporated. You may need more or less water, depending on the humidity in your kitchen. You can also make this in a food processor.

2. Start kneading the dough with both hands, primarily using the palms of your hands. Once the dough is a cohesive mass, remove the dough from the board and scrape up any leftover dry bits. Lightly flour the board and continue kneading for 3 more minutes. The dough should be elastic and a little sticky. Continue to knead for another 3 minutes, remembering to dust your board with flour when necessary. Wrap the dough in plastic wrap and set aside for 10 minutes at room temperature.

3. Roll dough into long dowels 3 to 4 inches thick. Cut into flat disks ¼ - to ½-inch thick. Press center of each disk with thumb to form saucer-shaped pasta and set aside until ready to cook. Bring a large pot of water to a rolling boil and season very generously with salt until it tastes like the sea. Cook the fresh orecchiette for 2 to 3 minutes or until al dente. Drain.

TO MAKE THE SAUCE:

4. In a large skillet, heat the olive oil over medium-high heat; then add the beans, celery, and chilies to the pan and let them sit. Cook for 2 minutes, then lay the onions on top and do not disturb the pan. After 2 more minutes, toss the ingredients in the pan and season with salt and red pepper flakes. Sauté for 2 to 3 more minutes. Then add the pasta, and a ladle or two of pasta water. Add the fresh caciocavallo cheese and serve.

Italian-Style Ham

Serves: 5   Skill Level: **Moderate**   Prep Time: **1 hour**   Cook Time: **3 ½ hours**
Inactive Prep Time: **12 hours**

Nothing says holiday like a ham, and you know what? It's a holiday when you say it's a holiday. An anniversary celebration is as worthy a time as any to serve up a deliciously caramelized slab of meat. The ingredients are simple, and so is the process: it's all about getting your pan hot enough to sear that ham and give you that beautiful crust. If you can't handle the heat, you're not doing your ham steak justice. Go high-octane and let it crackle!

FOR THE BRINE:

5 ½ cups kosher salt

6 cups packed light brown sugar

¼ cup, plus 2 tablespoons fennel seeds

¾ cup crushed black peppercorns

FOR THE HAM:

1, 6- to 8-pound bone-in leg of pork (shank end), often called a "fresh ham"

1 cup fresh sage leaves (from about 2 large bunches)

12 garlic cloves, peeled

¼ cup fennel pollen or ground toasted fennel seeds

3 tablespoons kosher salt

2 tablespoons freshly ground black pepper

¼ cup extra-virgin olive oil

TO MAKE THE BRINE:

1. Combine 6 cups water, kosher salt, and brown sugar in a large saucepan and heat over high heat, stirring, until the salt and sugar dissolve. Remove from the heat and pour into a pot or other container that is large enough to hold the pork and the brine. Add the fennel seeds and peppercorns, and set aside to cool while you prepare the roast.

TO MAKE THE HAM:

2. Using a very sharp, serrated knife, score a series of parallel lines one inch apart in the skin of the ham, making them about a ½-inch deep. Then score another series of parallel lines diagonally across the first cuts to make a diamond pattern.

3. Add 10 cups ice water to the brine mixture. Make sure the brine is completely cold before you add the ham. Submerge the ham in the brine, cover the container, and refrigerate for 12 hours; then remove and pat dry.

4. Preheat the oven to 350°F. Combine the sage, garlic, fennel pollen, kosher salt, pepper, and olive oil in a food processor and process until smooth, about 1 minute. Rub this mixture into the nooks and crannies in the surface of the ham.

5. Place the ham on a rack in a roasting pan, and bake in the oven for 3 hours, or until the internal temperature reaches 150°F.

FOR THE GLAZE:

1 cup packed light brown sugar

1 cup apple cider vinegar

½ cup apricot jam

2 tablespoons mustard powder

2 tablespoons anise seeds

TO MAKE THE GLAZE:

6. Meanwhile, make the glaze. Combine the brown sugar, cider vinegar, apricot jam, mustard powder, and anise seeds in a medium saucepan and bring to a boil, stirring to dissolve the sugar. Reduce the heat and simmer until reduced to 1½ cups and syrupy. Pour into a bowl and set aside.

7. When the pork has reached 150°F, brush on a thin layer of the glaze. Continue cooking, brushing often with glaze, until the internal temperature reaches 165°F. Transfer the pork to a carving board and allow it to rest for 15 minutes. Slice and serve.

Mario is rapt as Nigella Lawson—his culinary crush—shares some of her sage cooking advice.

Caramelized Carrots with Quinoa

Serves: 8   Skill Level: **Easy**   Prep Time: **15 minutes**   Cook Time: **25 minutes**

When you're cooking to entertain, it's easy to run out of oven space. But here's a dish that stays out of the way. All you need to whip up this quinoa dish is the stovetop, and things really start getting good when you caramelize those carrots. A dash of cumin adds some earthy flavor, and once you top it all off with vinaigrette, you've got a gorgeous, healthy dish made with one of my favorite grains on the planet!

FOR THE DRESSING:

Juice of half an orange

2 tablespoons red wine vinegar

1 tablespoon Dijon mustard

1 tablespoon real maple syrup

½ cup olive oil

Salt and freshly ground black pepper, to taste

¼ cup dried cherries

FOR THE QUINOA:

2 pounds carrots, peeled and cut at bias into ½-inch pieces

2 tablespoons olive oil

Salt and freshly ground black pepper, to taste

½ teaspoon ground cinnamon

1 teaspoon ground cumin

¼ teaspoon ground coriander

1 cup dry red quinoa, cooked to package instructions

2 scallions, sliced on bias, for garnish

¼ cup goat cheese, crumbled, for garnish

Toasted pumpkin seeds, for garnish

TO MAKE THE DRESSING:

1. In a large bowl, whisk together the orange juice, red wine vinegar, Dijon mustard, and maple syrup. Whisk in the olive oil in a steady stream. Season with salt and pepper to taste. Add the dried cherries and allow them to plump while you prepare the carrots and quinoa.

TO MAKE THE QUINOA:

2. Heat a cast-iron skillet over medium-high heat. Place the carrots in a large bowl, toss with olive oil, and then pour into cast-iron pan. Cook the carrots undisturbed for 2 minutes, allowing them to caramelize. Season with salt and pepper. Cook for 10 minutes and then add the cinnamon, cumin, and coriander. Combine until fragrant. Lower heat to low and cook until carrots are tender.

3. Add cooked carrots and quinoa to the bowl containing the vinaigrette. Toss to coat, and then top with scallions, crumbled goat cheese, and toasted pumpkin seeds. Serve warm.

DAPHNE
Having people over should be fun. You need to keep it simple and give yourself a couple of easy strategies. It's a party.

Coconut Layer Cake

Serves: **12**   Skill Level: **Moderate**   Prep Time: **30 minutes**   Cook Time: **12 to 15 minutes**

You know, since I'm a dessert diva, people are always asking me, "Carla, what's your favorite dessert?" Well, I'm finally ready to spill: it's coconut layer cake. This is a delicious treat coated with sweetened, shredded goodness, and it's the perfect ending to absolutely any occasion. In fact, the next time I'm invited to Mario's house for dinner, this is exactly what I'm going to bring for dessert! No question. It's that good. Are you as excited as I am?

FOR THE FROSTING:

2 cups granulated sugar

2 pints sour cream

6 cups flaked coconut

FOR THE CAKE:

2 cups cake flour, whisked

1½ cups granulated sugar

1 tablespoon baking powder

1 teaspoon salt

⅓ cup vegetable or canola oil

4 tablespoons unsalted butter

2 eggs

3 egg yolks

⅓ cup buttermilk

1 tablespoon vanilla extract

1 tablespoon spiced rum, optional

½ cup heavy cream, whipped to soft peaks

TO MAKE THE FROSTING:

1. Stir the granulated sugar, sour cream, and flaked coconut together in a medium bowl. Cover with plastic wrap and chill in the fridge overnight.

TO MAKE THE CAKE:

2. Preheat oven to 350°F. Grease and flour three 9-inch cake pans. Have all ingredients at room temperature. Add the flour, sugar, baking powder, and salt to the bowl of a standing mixer fitted with a paddle attachment. Mix on low for 30 seconds to combine. Stir in the oil and softened butter. Mix until combined.

3. Whisk the eggs, egg yolks, buttermilk, vanilla, and rum together in a separate bowl. Pour into bowl of mixer and mix on medium speed until the ingredients are combined thoroughly, about 2 minutes. Gently fold in the whipped heavy cream.

4. Divide the batter evenly among prepared cake pans, about 1⅓ cups batter per pan. Bake in the center of the oven for 12 to 15 minutes, until the cake springs back in center when touched or a toothpick comes out clean. Let the cakes cool for 10 minutes, then turn out onto baking racks. Let cool completely before decorating.

5. Place one layer of the cake on a plate and spread about one quarter of the frosting on top. Add a second layer of cake and spread on another quarter of the frosting. Top with a third layer of cake and cover top and sides with remaining frosting. Allow cake to chill in the fridge until ready to serve, up to three days.

BIG BASH

When it's time to pull out all the stops and celebrate like you really *mean* it, you're probably about to throw a "Big Bash." The Big Bash can take several different forms, but they all have one thing in common: they all share the spirit of "Go big or go home!" Now, that doesn't mean you have to have a party with more people than your space can reasonably hold, but it does mean that you're going to dress up, ask your guests to do the same, and make a few hors d'oeuvres, sides, and entrées that are not part of your everyday repertoire. The Big Bash is the ultimate in eat, drink, and be merry. And dance, if you are so inclined. These cocktails and delectable edibles will help you get your party started right.

AWARDS NIGHT

Oscar-rita

Serves: **2**   Skill Level: **Easy**   Prep Time: **5 minutes**

Awards nights just scream "cocktail party!" There's no way to watch the Oscars, Tonys, Emmys, Grammys, or Independent Spirit Awards while you're eating a sit-down dinner! So if you're having a cocktail party, you've got to start with the right cocktail. We've already introduced you to the Psychorita for Halloween; now I'd like you to meet the Oscar-rita. (Who is this Rita person?) The Oscar-rita features the tequila of a margarita with the golden hue of pineapple juice. Just hold your glass in front of you and you'll feel like you're holding an award of your own. And you kind of are.

3 tablespoons fresh mint leaves

¼ cup silver tequila

¼ cup pineapple juice

3 tablespoons lime juice

Seltzer, to top off

Muddle the mint in a mixing glass. Add the tequila, pineapple juice, and lime juice, and stir to mix. Pour over ice in a margarita glass and top off with seltzer.

CLINTON
Don't ask your guests to bring their own alcohol. If you're on a budget, you can make your alcohol go a long way by mixing a signature cocktail like a punch. And you can pick up a bunch of very inexpensive wines to serve once the good stuff is gone. Your guests won't even know the difference.

Cauliflower Fritters

Serves: 15   Skill Level: **Easy**   Prep Time: **10 minutes**   Cook Time: **25 to 30 minutes**

When you want to make something elegant as a party snack but don't want to spend much money, what do you do? You make these cauliflower fritters! You probably already have most of the ingredients at home; at most you'll have to spring for two heads of cauliflower. Not so bad, right? Fry these babies up, plate them on a silver(ish) platter (use a little decorative paper to soak up any excess oil), and stick in those toothpicks. Fried goodies like this are the first to disappear at a party, so make sure you eat a few before they leave the kitchen!

FOR THE SPICY VINAIGRETTE:

3 teaspoons sriracha hot sauce

1 teaspoon mustard

2 teaspoons rice wine vinegar

1/4 cup cilantro, leaves only

1/4 cup olive oil

1 teaspoon salt

FOR THE FRITTERS:

1 cup water

1 teaspoon kosher salt

1/2 cup unsalted butter

1 cup all-purpose flour

5 eggs

Freshly ground black pepper

2 small heads of cauliflower, about 1 1/2 pounds, cut into 1-inch florets

2 quarts olive oil, for deep-frying

Salt, to taste

TO MAKE THE SPICY VINAIGRETTE:

1. Combine all ingredients in a blender and puree until smooth. Pour into a small bowl or ramekin.

TO MAKE THE FRITTERS:

2. Combine the water, salt, and butter in a 2-quart saucepan and bring to a boil. Have a whisk and a wooden spoon ready. Remove the pan from the heat and add the flour all at once, whisking it in. Return to the heat and start stirring with the wooden spoon. Cook, stirring constantly, until the dough starts to pull from the sides of the pan and form a ball, about 3 minutes. Remove from the heat and stir until tepid, 6 to 8 minutes. Add the eggs, one at a time, incorporating each one completely before adding the next. Crack about 20 turns of black pepper into the batter. Pour into a mixing bowl, cover with plastic wrap, and set aside at room temperature.

3. Prepare an ice bath containing 3 cups of ice and 4 cups of water. In a medium pot, bring 4 quarts of water to a boil. Place the cauliflower into the boiling water and cook until tender (not al dente), 8 to 10 minutes. Remove with slotted spoon and transfer to ice bath. Drain the cauliflower pieces well and dry on a kitchen towel. Add the cauliflower to the batter and stir gently to mix well.

4. Heat the oil to 375°F in a 6- to 8-quart pot. Line a baking sheet with several layers of paper towels and preheat the oven to 200°F. Using 2 tablespoons, form fritters by grabbing a floret of cauliflower with a

generous amount of the batter that adheres. Drop the fritter into the hot oil. Cook 6 or 7 at a time until golden brown, flipping them with a slotted spoon. Remove to the prepared baking sheet, season with salt, and keep warm in the oven while you fry the remaining fritters. Serve hot with the spicy vinaigrette.

Oysters Rockefeller

Serves: 8   Skill Level: **Moderate**   Prep Time: **20 minutes**   Cook Time: **10 to 15 minutes**

If you want your party to be a little fancy, one of the obvious choices is to serve oysters. Oysters always seem to come out to play when a luxurious feast is being put together. Another way to make your party fancy is to drop a few famous names into the conversation. Who cares if the names you're dropping are of industry giants who haven't been around for over a century? In this country, Rockefeller still means classy! If you put "oyster" next to "Rockefeller," you're serving up some double-barreled elegance. The good news is that oysters Rockefeller also happens to be insanely good eating. And they're so rich (calling Mr. Rockefeller again!), just a few go a very long way.

3 tablespoons butter

1 small onion, finely chopped

Salt, to taste

1 garlic clove, minced

4 cups fresh spinach

2 teaspoons anise-flavored liquor, optional

½ cup panko bread crumbs

⅓ cup grated Parmesan

Hot sauce, to taste

Freshly ground black pepper, to taste

16 large oysters, shucked and chilled in half shell

Rock salt, to line baking sheet

1. Preheat oven to 400°F.

2. Melt the butter in a sauté pan over medium heat. Add the onions and season with salt. Cook for 2 to 3 minutes, or until translucent. Add the garlic and cook until fragrant. Add the spinach and toss to combine with onions. Drizzle the anise liquor over spinach and cook until wilted. Remove pan from heat and stir in bread crumbs, Parmesan, and hot sauce. Adjust seasoning to taste.

3. Place a heaping tablespoon of spinach mixture on top of each oyster and arrange on a baking sheet lined with rock salt. Bake for 6 to 8 minutes or until light gold on top. Serve warm with a glass of cold champagne.

PROD .NO. THE CHEW

SCENE	TAKE	ROLL

DATE	SOUND
PROD .CO.	
DIRECTOR	
CAMERAMAN	

Beef Skewers with Cilantro Pesto

Serves: **4**   Skill Level: **Easy**   Prep Time: **20 minutes**   Cook Time: **5 to 8 minutes**
Inactive Prep Time: **30 minutes**

These beef skewers are great for a dinner party or a cocktail party, whatever suits you best. They are standouts because they're both delicious and versatile. The marinated beef can stay on its skewers to be served with rice for a sit-down meal (if you don't mind missing that middle portion of the awards show when they give away all the random honors). *Or*, you can take the cubes of beef off the skewers, stick cocktail picks in them, and serve them as individual bites (if you absolutely have to see the lifetime achievement presentation various awards shows interject).

8 wood or bamboo skewers

2 tablespoons olive oil

1 teaspoon coriander seeds

½ teaspoon crushed red pepper flakes

1 pound beef sirloin, cut into 1-inch cubes

Kosher salt and freshly ground black pepper, to taste

2 cups fresh cilantro leaves

2 garlic cloves, roughly chopped

¼ cup roughly chopped, toasted hazelnuts

½ cup Parmesan

½ cup extra-virgin olive oil

1. Preheat a grill or grill pan to medium-high heat. If using a grill, soak the skewers in cold water for 30 minutes.

2. In a medium bowl, whisk together the olive oil, coriander, and red pepper flakes. Season the beef with salt and black pepper. Add the beef pieces to the marinade and toss to coat. Divide the beef into eight portions and thread the meat onto each of the eight skewers.

3. Put the beef skewers on the grill, cover, and cook for 3 minutes. Flip the beef and cook until the meat is well caramelized, about 2 minutes.

4. Meanwhile, in a blender or food processor, combine the cilantro, garlic, hazelnuts, Parmesan, and extra-virgin olive oil. Process until smooth. Taste and adjust the seasoning, adding salt as needed.

5. Remove the skewers from the grill and put on a platter. Drizzle with some of the cilantro pesto and serve the rest on the side as a dipping sauce. Serve immediately.

Spicy Pork Meatball Lettuce Cups

Serves: 8 to 10   Skill Level: **Moderate**   Prep Time: **20 minutes**   Cook Time: **8 to 10 minutes**

Don't you just hate it when you have to get up in the middle of your favorite actor's acceptance speech to go wash grease off your hands? Gotta love party fare that you can just pop in your mouth with no mess left behind. What's even *better* is if your cocktail bite comes in a wrapper you can *eat*. So it is with these meatballs in lettuce cups. The meatballs come packed with flavor, thanks to all the aromatics, spices, and sauces that go in the mix. And the lettuce cups cool all that heat down a little and keep your hands clean. Mouthwatering, pleasing to the eye, and *tidy*. Perfect.

FOR THE SPICY PORK MEATBALLS:

½ cup day-old bread, finely chopped or torn

½ cup whole milk

1 pound ground pork

½ cup onion, minced

2 cloves garlic, minced

1 jalapeño, seeded, stem removed, and minced

½ teaspoon ground coriander

1 teaspoon fish sauce, optional

Zest of 1 orange

Salt and freshly ground black pepper, to taste

Flour, for dredging

Canola oil, for panfrying

TO MAKE THE MEATBALLS:

1. In a small bowl, soak the bread in the milk.

2. In the meantime, in a large mixing bowl combine pork, onion, garlic, jalapeño, coriander, fish sauce, and orange zest. Season well with salt and pepper. Allow the excess milk to drip off the bread and add it to the meat mixture, discarding the remaining milk. Mix well, then form into golf ball–sized meatballs.

3. Heat a large sauté pan over medium-high heat. When the pan is hot, add enough canola oil to come 1 inch up the sides of the pan. Dredge the meatballs in the flour, shaking off any excess, then place them in the pan. Brown on all sides until cooked through, 8 to 10 minutes. Then remove to paper towels and assemble your lettuce cups.

TO ASSEMBLE THE LETTUCE CUPS:

4. Choose the bigger outer leaves of lettuce. Place two meatballs in each followed by a piece of cucumber, some radishes, carrot, mint, and cilantro; then top with jalapeño. Garnish with lime wedges.

MICHAEL
It's not the Oscars, but at the James Beard Awards—the time that I won—the first thing I said when I walked up there was, "I'd like to thank Liz." And then I figured anything else that happens after that is fine. Thank the wife first, always.

1 head Bibb lettuce, leaves separated

1 English cucumber, julienned or cut into 2-inch strips

4 radishes, sliced

½ cup shredded carrots

¼ cup mint leaves, torn

¼ cup cilantro leaves, picked

1 jalapeño, seeded, stem removed, and sliced into rings

1 lime, cut in wedges

Chocolate Mousse with Tuile

Serves: **36**   Skill Level: **Moderate**   Prep Time: **30 minutes**   Cook Time: **20 minutes**

This dessert is totally elegant, and elegance is a must when you're watching a red-carpet event. At the same time, these mini treats are cocktail party–friendly and just so darned *cute!* When you're serving food to people who are standing up (or at least not sitting at a table), making it manageable to eat is key. This decadent mousse with its crackly little cookie can be served in espresso cups (there's espresso in the recipe, so why not?) with demitasse spoons. Two or three bites and they'll all be gone, and your guests can move on to whatever else you've got planned for them!

FOR THE *TUILES*:

8 tablespoons unsalted butter

½ cup granulated sugar

⅓ cup light corn syrup

1½ cups almonds, finely ground

1 tablespoon cocoa powder

1 tablespoon flour

½ teaspoon salt

1 teaspoon vanilla extract

CARLA

Tuile means "tile" in French. These cookies are meant to be reminiscent of the clay roofing tiles used in France, which are a lovely red-brown color and curved, just like these *tuiles*. If you're feeling Gallic next Christmas, try using these cookies to roof your gingerbread house!

TO MAKE THE *TUILES*:

1. In a large saucepot, stir together the butter, sugar, and corn syrup over low heat. When the butter has melted and mixture is thoroughly combined, add the almonds, cocoa, flour, salt, and vanilla, and stir to combine. Transfer the batter to a heatproof bowl and allow to cool to room temperature. This can be made up to two weeks in advance and stored, refrigerated, in an airtight container.

2. Preheat oven to 350°F. Line a baking sheet with a silicone baking mat or parchment paper. Form five, 1-inch balls of batter and place on the baking sheet, leaving about 3 inches between each. Dampen a spatula or finger with water and flatten the balls into thin 3-inch discs. Bake for 5 to 6 minutes. When working in batches, the cook time may decrease slightly if the pan does not cool off completely before starting the next batch.

3. To shape the *tuiles*, use an offset spatula to transfer the hot cookies immediately to a small glass bowl or drape over a rolling pin. Gently press to shape, then allow the cookies to cool completely. Store in an airtight container until ready to use.

FOR THE MOUSSE:

4 ounces bittersweet chocolate, chopped

2 tablespoons unsalted butter

2 tablespoons strong coffee or espresso

2 large eggs, yolks and whites separated

2 tablespoons almond liqueur

⅛ teaspoon cream of tartar

6 tablespoons sugar, divided

1 teaspoon vanilla extract

1 cup heavy cream

Toasted sliced almonds, for garnish

Chocolate shavings, for garnish

TO MAKE THE MOUSSE:

4. Place a heatproof bowl over a pot of gently simmering water, making sure that the bowl does not touch the surface of the water. Combine chocolate, butter, and espresso in the bowl and stir until melted. Mix in the egg yolks, and then the almond liqueur. Cover and set aside. In a stand mixer or using a hand mixer, whip the egg whites and cream of tartar until foamy, then gradually add 2 tablespoons of sugar and continue to whip until stiff peaks form, yet the whites are still glossy and not dry. Set aside.

5. In another bowl, whip the heavy cream, remaining sugar, and vanilla extract until soft peaks form. Mix a few spoonfuls of the egg white mixture into the chocolate mixture, and then gently fold the remaining egg whites into the chocolate mixture until thoroughly combined. Fold in half of the whipped cream. Place a large spoonful of mousse into the *tuile* and top with a dollop of the remaining whipped cream, almonds, and chocolate shavings. This can be made a day ahead and chilled in the fridge.

Mini Cannoli

Serves: **12**   Skill Level: **Easy**   Prep Time: **15 minutes**   Inactive Cook Time: **2 to 4 hours**

CARLA: And the award goes to . . . mini desserts. Why? Because you don't have to share! These mini cannoli are just like the big guys, but they make up for being teeny tiny by packing an extra punch in the filling. Pistachios, cherries, and limoncello make your taste buds stand up and say, *"Hello!"* when you launch one of these minis into your mouth.

DAPHNE: Some desserts might claim that it's an honor just to be nominated, but take one taste of my mini cannoli and you'll know they are winners. I've added cocoa powder and a few other surprises to the standard cannoli filling so no one has to choose between this Italian classic and a chocolate treat. Unless you want both . . . then go right ahead!

FOR THE CANNOLI FILLING BASE:

2 cups ricotta

1 cup mascarpone, room temperature

¾ cup confectioners' sugar, plus more for garnish

¼ teaspoon salt

1 teaspoon vanilla

FOR CARLA'S CANNOLI FILLING:

¼ cup limoncello

½ cup dried cherries, chopped

½ cup pistachios, plus more for garnish

1 lemon, zested

Confectioners' sugar

TO MAKE THE CANNOLI FILLING BASE:

1. Set the ricotta over a fine-mesh strainer and allow to drain for 2 to 4 hours.

2. In a large bowl, mix together the strained ricotta, mascarpone, sugar, salt, and vanilla. Stir until smooth.

TO MAKE CARLA'S CANNOLI:

3. In a small bowl, combine the limoncello with the chopped cherries. Allow to rehydrate for 10 minutes, then drain.

4. Fold the pistachios, cherries, and lemon zest into the filling base. Place the cannoli filling in a large piping bag. Pipe the filling into the mini cannoli shells. Sprinkle with confectioners' sugar, garnish with chopped pistachios, and serve.

> **CARLA**
> I did theater from when I was twelve until I was seventeen, and still, to this very day, have dreams of being on the stage or the screen.

**FOR DAPHNE'S
CANNOLI FILLING:**

¼ cup unsweetened cocoa
powder

½ cup hazelnuts, toasted

½ cup coconut, toasted

Confectioners' sugar

⅓ cup mini chocolate chips,
for garnish

FOR ASSEMBLY:

24 store-bought mini
cannoli shells

TO MAKE DAPHNE'S CANNOLI:

3. Fold the cocoa powder, hazelnuts, and coconut into the filling base. Place the cannoli filling in a large piping bag. Pipe the filling into mini cannoli shells.

4. Sprinkle with confectioners' sugar, garnish with mini chocolate chips, and serve.

ELEGANT DINNER PARTY

Sazerac

Serves: **1**   Skill Level: **Easy**   Prep Time: **5 minutes**

Born in New Orleans and now enjoyed all over the United States, the Sazerac is the king of cocktails. It's as potent as it gets, has a unique flavor, and features absinthe. Why is it cool that Sazerac cocktails have absinthe in them? Because until about a decade ago, absinthe was illegal in the United States and many European countries. It had the reputation of being the drink of choice for painters (like van Gogh) and poets (like Rimbaud) and was the final straw that drove them mad. Absinthe has shaken its bad-boy image over the years and is now widely available. Which means you can finally make an authentic Sazerac at home. Drink up!

FOR THE SIMPLE SYRUP:

1 cup granulated sugar

1 cup water

FOR THE SAZERAC:

1 tablespoon simple syrup

Dash of bitters

⅓ cup rye whiskey

½ ounce absinthe

Lemon peel, to garnish

TO MAKE THE SIMPLE SYRUP:

1. Place the sugar and the water in a small saucepan and bring to a boil. Cook until the sugar has dissolved, about 5 minutes. Cool and store in an airtight container for up to two weeks. Makes 1 cup simple syrup.

TO MAKE THE SAZERAC:

2. Fill a glass with ice to chill.

3. Pour the simple syrup, bitters, and whiskey into a shaker with ice and shake vigorously to chill.

4. Remove ice from the chilled glass and add absinthe. Swirl to coat interior of glass, then discard both ice and excess absinthe.

5. Strain cocktail into chilled glass.

6. Twist lemon peel to garnish.

Leek, Parsnip, and Carrot Agnolotti in Brodo

Serves: 8   Skill Level: **Difficult**   Prep Time: **1 hour**   Cook Time: **20 to 25 minutes**

Hailing from the Piedmont region of Italy, agnolotti is a classic dish very similar to ravioli. Agnolotti are traditionally stuffed with a mixture of meat and vegetables, but this version uses only vegetables (yet is every bit as tasty). The vegetables used are available all year round, so this warming appetizer or main course can be served whenever the mood strikes you.

3 tablespoons extra-virgin olive oil

2 medium carrots, peeled and sliced into ¼-inch coins

1 parsnip, peeled and cut into ¼-inch pieces

Salt, to taste

1 leek, cut in half lengthwise, thinly sliced, and rinsed thoroughly (with tough greens discarded)

⅓ cup ricotta, drained

⅓ cup grated Italian Fontina

¼ cup freshly grated Parmesan

¼ cup Italian parsley, chopped, plus more for garnish

1 tablespoon fresh thyme leaves, chopped

¼ teaspoon freshly grated nutmeg

Freshly ground black pepper

6 cups chicken stock

1½ pounds fresh pasta sheets

1. Heat olive oil in a large pan over medium-high heat. Sauté the carrots and parsnips, seasoning with salt, for 2 minutes. Toss in the leeks and cook until translucent, about 3 minutes. Remove from heat and transfer to a food processor. Puree until smooth. Set aside to cool to room temperature. Once the vegetable mixture is cool, stir in the cheeses, herbs, and spices. Adjust seasoning to taste.

2. Heat the stock in a Dutch oven over medium heat. Lay the pasta sheets on a cutting board, cutting into two, 2- x 3-inch rectangles. Place a tablespoon of filling in the center of each rectangle. Brush the edges of the dough with water, then fold in half. Press the edges to seal, pushing out any air pockets. You should end up with small rectangles of agnolotti.

3. Place the agnolotti in boiling stock and cook for 3 to 4 minutes, or until pasta is cooked to al dente. Use a slotted spoon to portion out the agnolotti into bowls. Ladle broth over top and garnish with parsley.

MARIO
Reduce the stress of your party. You should do dishes that don't need a lot of last-minute attention. Do things that can sit for half an hour and will not be wrecked. You don't need to paint the plates with the sauces to make it feel like a party.

Red Cabbage and Apple Salad

Serves: **8**   Skill Level: **Easy**   Prep Time: **20 minutes**

This salad has it all: wildly healthy ingredients, great crunchy texture, and a sweet-and-sour dressing that will make even your pickiest eaters dig in to a serving of cabbage with gusto. At *The Chew* we always have our eye on making our food beautiful, tasty, and cost-effective. The ingredients in this salad hit all our criteria. We hope you and your dinner guests love this *agrodolce* (Italian for sweet-and-sour) and very versatile side dish or appetizer as much as we do.

½ cup golden raisins

⅓ cup apple cider vinegar

Juice and zest of 1 orange, divided

1 tablespoon brown mustard

¼ cup olive oil

Salt and freshly ground black pepper, to taste

½ head red cabbage, thinly sliced

2 red beets, scrubbed clean and grated

1 large Granny Smith apple, julienned

½ red onion, very thinly sliced

⅓ cup pumpkin seeds, toasted

1. Soak the raisins in the vinegar and the juice from half the orange for 10 minutes. Strain and add the soaking liquid to a large bowl. Whisk in the orange zest, juice from the other half of the orange, mustard, and olive oil. Season with salt and pepper and adjust to taste.

2. Add the cabbage, beets, apple, onion, and golden raisins. Toss to coat and then taste, adjusting seasoning if necessary. Serve, topped with toasted pumpkin seeds.

DAPHNE
Plan your party in stages. Have something in the oven and have something that is served cold so you're not standing by the stove, hovering and stressing yourself out.

Beef Wellington

Serves: 10   Skill Level: **Difficult**   Prep Time: **10 minutes**   Cook Time: **1 hour, 15 minutes**

Thanks to PBS and the BBC, when we think "elegant dinner party," one of the things we think of is "British upper crust." Following that logic, there can't be any dish more suited to an elegant dinner party than beef Wellington, supposedly named after the First Duke of Wellington. Aside from specious associations like that one, this is indeed a famously popular main course for fancy dinner parties. The ingredients and taste are so very decadent, and when assembled with care before going in the oven, a beef Wellington can look very impressive when it arrives at the table. This is a particularly rich offering where a small serving can go a long way, so don't be nervous about serving thinner slices to start.

3-pound beef tenderloin, fat trimmed

Salt and freshly ground black pepper, to taste

3 tablespoons extra-virgin olive oil

4 tablespoons butter, divided

2 shallots, minced

2 garlic cloves, minced

1½ pounds button mushrooms, minced

3 fresh thyme sprigs, leaves pulled

2 sheets frozen puff pastry, thawed

⅓ cup English mustard

1 egg, plus 1 tablespoon of water, whisked

¼ cup red wine

½ cup beef stock

1 tablespoon crème fraîche

1. Preheat the oven to 425°F. Line a baking sheet with parchment paper. Remove steak from the fridge and let come to room temperature, about 30 minutes before you're ready to cook it.

2. Season steak with a generous amount of salt and pepper. Heat a large sauté pan over medium-high heat. Add olive oil to the pan and sear meat on all sides until golden brown, about 10 minutes. Drain the excess fat from the pan.

3. Heat another large sauté pan over medium-high heat and add 3 tablespoons of the butter. Once the butter is melted and foamy, add the shallots and a pinch of salt and cook for 2 to 3 minutes, until softened. Add the garlic and cook just until fragrant, about 1 minute. Add the mushrooms and thyme, season with salt and pepper, and toss to incorporate. Sauté for 5 minutes, stirring occasionally, until the mushrooms are cooked and there is little moisture remaining in the pan. Remove from heat and allow to cool.

CLINTON
Adult parties should be
relaxed, social affairs.
Chances are not all of your
guests want to play a game.
If you want, you can set out
a few conversation-starting
party games for people to
pursue at their leisure.

4. Roll out the pastry on a lightly floured surface to 3 to 4 inches longer and 5 to 6 inches wider than the tenderloin. Brush with the mustard and spread the cooled mushroom mixture on the pastry, leaving a 1-inch border. Place the tenderloin in the center of the pastry. Fold the dough around the beef to cover completely and seal by pressing gently. Transfer to the prepared baking sheet, seam-side down. Brush with the egg wash and season with salt. Bake for 30 to 35 minutes, until the pastry is a nice golden brown and the internal temperature reaches 125°F to 130°F for medium-rare. Remove from pan and allow to rest for 10 to 15 minutes before slicing.

5. Return the original sauté pan to the stove and set over medium heat. Once hot, deglaze with red wine, scraping up the crispy bits with a wooden spoon. Whisk beef stock, remaining butter, and the crème fraîche just until warm and emulsified. Adjust the seasoning to taste and serve over sliced tenderloin.

Brown Butter Mash

Serves: **4 to 6**　　　Skill Level: **Easy**　　　Prep Time: **15 minutes**　　　Cook Time: **35 to 40 minutes**

Butter is a really versatile ingredient. It's essential to baking, makes just about everything it touches creamy and addictively good, and even acts as a thickener for sauces and stews. Another thing it does is add flavor. We all know what regular butter tastes like (we love it melted over baked potatoes, popcorn, and lobster to name a few of the usual suspects), but its flavor can be changed with nothing more than heat. When you brown butter in a pan, it takes on a nuttiness that adds depth to whatever it goes into. Without changing the ingredients for regular mashed potatoes, browning the butter makes a whole new recipe.

2 pounds Russet potatoes, peeled and cut into 2-inch cubes

Kosher salt

1 cup unsalted butter, cut into tablespoon-sized pieces

1. Place potatoes into a large pot and fill with enough cold water to cover. Season with a large pinch of kosher salt and bring to a boil. Reduce heat to a simmer and cook for 25 minutes, until potatoes are very tender. Drain and return to pot.

2. In a heavy-bottomed skillet, heat ½ cup butter over medium heat until it foams and subsides. Whisk as it cooks and brown bits begin to form. Remove from heat immediately when butter has browned and taken a nutty flavor, being mindful not to burn.

3. Using a potato masher, mash the potatoes along with the browned butter and remaining ½ cup butter. Once smooth, serve.

Citrus Upside-Down Cake

Serves: **8**   Skill Level: **Easy**   Prep Time: **20 minutes**   Cook Time: **40 minutes**

This dessert is a no-brainer. It's so gorgeous that when you bring it to the table everyone will go, "Oooh! Aaah! Where did you get that?" And you'll say, "My own kitchen, thank you very much!" No need to reveal that it's actually pretty easy to make. This is a new take on the classic pineapple upside-down cake, using blood oranges and lemons instead of pineapple for more vivid and contrasting color as well as a bright, fresh flavor instead of the usually overwhelming sweetness of the original.

1 cup, plus 3 tablespoons unsalted butter, at room temperature, divided

2/3 cup packed light brown sugar

2 Meyer lemons, 1 juiced and 1 whole

3 blood oranges

1½ cups all-purpose flour

1½ teaspoons baking powder

1 teaspoon salt

1 cup sugar

4 large eggs, at room temperature

1/3 cup sour cream

2 teaspoons vanilla extract

Soft whipped cream, for garnish

Powdered sugar, for garnish

1. Preheat the oven to 350°F. Grease a 9-inch-round cake pan. In a small saucepan over medium heat, melt 3 tablespoons of butter. Add the brown sugar and lemon juice and stir until everything is dissolved, 2 to 3 minutes. Scrape this mixture into the bottom of the prepared pan.

2. Grate a ½ teaspoon of zest from the lemon and a ½ teaspoon of zest from one of the oranges and set aside; then slice off the tops and bottoms of all four pieces of fruit. Place the fruit on a clean, flat surface, and slice away the rind and pith, top to bottom, following the curve of the fruit. Slice each fruit crosswise into ¼-inch-thick wheels; discard any seeds. Arrange wheels on top of brown sugar mixture in a single, tight layer. Use the blood orange slices on the outside rim and the lemon wheels on the inner circle.

3. In a large bowl, whisk together the citrus zest, flour, baking powder, and salt. In a separate bowl, whisk together 1 cup of butter and the sugar. Beat in the eggs, one at a time, then beat in the sour cream and vanilla. Stir in the flour mixture.

4. Pour the batter over the fruit in the cake pan. Transfer to the oven and bake until the cake is golden brown and a toothpick inserted into the center comes out clean, about 40 minutes.

5. Let rest in the cake pan for about 10 minutes. Then run a knife around the edges and invert the cake onto a platter. Cool completely before serving. Garnish with whipped cream and powdered sugar.

Drip-Dye Coasters

If you have even the remotest sense of good manners, you know that you never put a cold drink down on any surface without a coaster. Do you want to be the guest at someone's house who leaves rings on Great-Aunt Bertha's Chippendale tea table? Didn't think so! So if you're racking your brain for the perfect hostess gift when you're going to an elegant dinner party, give these a try. The technique lets you channel a little bit of your inner Jackson Pollock (if you've got a little inner Jackson Pollock, it's probably best for you to let him out anyway) and be the most gracious guest on the invitation list.

Paper towels

Rubbing alcohol

White tiles (4x4 inches for coasters, 6x6 inches for trivets)

Alcohol ink

Self-adhesive felt pads

Acrylic paint, optional

Clear sealing or finishing spray

1. Saturate a paper towel with rubbing alcohol. Rub your tile to clean, leaving a layer of rubbing alcohol on the surface of the tile.

2. While the alcohol is still wet, begin dropping ink on the tile. The ink will spread from the point of contact depending on how much alcohol is on the tile. Use your imagination to mix colors and create designs!

3. If you would like, you can paint the edges with acrylic paint for a clean look.

4. Allow to dry completely and coat with the sealing spray to set colors. Place the self-adhesive felt pads on the bottom of the coasters to keep from slipping or from scratching surfaces.

Shown at left with the Drip-Dye Coaster is Clinton's Blood Orange Party Punch. For the recipe, turn to page 231.

NEW YEAR'S EVE

Blood Orange Party Punch

Serves: **18 to 20**   Skill Level: **Moderate**   Prep Time: **10 minutes**   Inactive Cook Time: **12 hours**

When you're serving a lot of people, it's no fun if you've got to play bartender and spend the whole night mixing drinks. And when it's New Year's Eve and you really want to be kicking up your heels, getting trapped behind the bar is *the worst*. Fear not! There is a solution to this dilemma; all you've got to do is whip up a big bowl of punch (and keep that bowl full!), and everyone can serve him or herself. Including you!

FOR THE BLOOD ORANGE-INFUSED VODKA:

1 bottle vodka

Peel of 4 blood oranges, strips peeled with a peeler

FOR THE PUNCH:

8 cups blood orange juice

1 cup lime juice

3 cups blood orange–infused vodka

8 cups ginger ale

Lime wedges, to garnish

TO MAKE THE BLOOD ORANGE-INFUSED VODKA:

1. Combine the vodka and the blood orange peel in a large mason jar or other clean jar fitted with a lid. Place in the fridge and infuse overnight.

TO MAKE THE PUNCH:

2. Combine the blood orange juice, lime juice, and vodka with ice in a large punch bowl. Mix well. Add the ginger ale and garnish with lime wedges before serving.

CARLA
I don't make New Year's resolutions. I always try to feel present. Listening is a big part of being present.

Clinton gets a few pointers from flair bartender Chris Cardone.

Braised Leeks with Olive Oil Vinaigrette

Serves: 6   Skill Level: **Easy**   Prep Time: **25 to 30 minutes**   Cook Time: **35 to 40 minutes**

Here's another classic with a twist. Leeks dressed with vinaigrette appear in several different kinds of Mediterranean cuisine. What I've done to make this distinctive enough for the kickoff of a new year is to add a few ingredients to the vinaigrette that don't usually show up there: Pecorino, olives, and chili flakes. Serve this as a side dish or appetizer on December 31, and add it to your repertoire for the coming year. It's priced right and takes almost no time to put together.

FOR THE LEEKS:

6 leeks

3 tablespoons olive oil

Salt and freshly ground black pepper, to taste

1 cup white wine

4 tablespoons butter, cut into small cubes

1 cup water

4 sprigs thyme

3 garlic cloves, sliced thinly

1 cup shallots, sliced

FOR THE VINAIGRETTE:

1/3 cup black olives, pitted and roughly chopped

1/2 cup parsley, chopped

1 teaspoon chili flakes

4 tablespoons red wine vinegar

Salt and freshly ground black pepper, to taste

2 tablespoons olive oil

1/4 cup Pecorino

TO MAKE THE LEEKS:

1. Trim the roots of the leeks, leaving the root end intact. Trim off tops on diagonal, leaving 2 inches of light green. Cut in half lengthwise from white end to green end, leaving the root intact (the root holds the leeks together while cooking). Clean very well in water to remove internal grit. Pat dry with a towel.

2. Heat a large sauté pan over medium heat. Add olive oil and lay leeks in the pan without crowding them. Season with salt and pepper, then add the wine and butter. Bring to a simmer and reduce the liquid by half. Add the water, thyme, garlic, and shallots. Season again with a pinch of salt and ground black pepper if necessary. Bring to a boil and reduce to a simmer. Put a lid on and gently cook for 30 minutes, or until fork-tender.

TO MAKE THE VINAIGRETTE:

3. While the leeks are braising, make the vinaigrette. Combine the olives, parsley, chili flakes, and red wine vinegar in a small bowl. Season with salt and pepper, and then pour in the olive oil. The vinaigrette should not be fully combined; it is not necessary to emulsify. Grate the Pecorino into the vinaigrette.

4. Dress the cooked leeks with the fresh vinaigrette and serve.

Spanish Shrimp Romesco

Serves: 4   Skill Level: **Easy**   Prep Time: **20 minutes**   Cook Time: **10 to 15 minutes**

Sometimes you just have to pull out the big guns to impress. In this case, replace the word "guns" with "shrimp." It may not have the same ring to it, but trust me when I say that this is a dish with major impact. Oh, and the whole operation takes less than twenty minutes. Not bad, right? This Romesco sauce is sweet, spicy, and smoky, with a smooth creaminess added by the almonds. It's the perfect accompaniment to the grilled shrimp, which have a delicate taste that shouldn't be overwhelmed.

FOR THE ROMESCO SAUCE:

1 cup olive oil

3 red bell peppers, roughly chopped

2 Fresno chilies, chopped

½ head garlic, smashed and peeled

2 ripe tomatoes, halved

¼ cup slivered almonds

1½ cups stale bread, cubed

Salt, to taste

1 teaspoon smoked paprika

½ cup red wine vinegar

Juice and zest of 1 orange

FOR THE SHRIMP:

12 colossal head-on shrimp

Salt and freshly ground black pepper

Extra-virgin olive oil, for brushing

TO MAKE THE ROMESCO SAUCE:

1. In a large Dutch oven, heat 1 cup of olive oil over medium heat. Add the peppers, Fresno chilies, garlic, tomatoes, almonds, and bread. Season with the salt and smoked paprika. Cook on the stove for 6 to 10 minutes.

2. Remove from heat and transfer to a blender or food processor (this can be done in batches if necessary). Add the red wine vinegar, orange zest and juice, and season again with salt, if necessary. Puree sauce until smooth.

TO MAKE THE SHRIMP:

3. Preheat a griddle or cast-iron skillet over high heat, and brush with olive oil. Season the shrimp with salt and pepper, and then arrange on the griddle or skillet.

4. Cook until pink, about 5 minutes per side. Serve with the Romesco sauce.

MICHAEL
Four or five years ago, Liz and I decided to always spend New Year's Eve together. I cook a very simple meal, usually crab legs with steamed artichoke. We sit in front of a fire, we chill, and it's just a Liz-and-I night.

Mario makes a bubbly treat for
Star Trek legend George Takei.

BBQ Lamb Chops

Serves: 6   **Skill Level: Easy**   **Prep Time: 10 minutes**   **Cook Time: 4 to 6 minutes**
Inactive Prep Time: 30 minutes

These lamb chops couldn't be simpler to make. Which is good for two reasons: nobody wants to be stuck in the kitchen on New Year's Eve, and, easy plus delectable equals *SCORE!* The secret to these lamb chops is twofold. First, get the best lamb chops you can from your local grocery store or butcher. Good-quality meat is always important. Second, the marinade for a barbecue like this is essential. The more complex the flavor, the better. This marinade is sweet, sour, salty, and herbal. A little bit of everything that gives grilled meat, particularly lamb, that "wow" factor. A pretty good way to start off the year, no?

2 tablespoons olive oil

2 tablespoons red wine vinegar

3 tablespoons sugar

2 sprigs mint, leaves removed and chopped

2 sprigs rosemary, leaves removed and chopped

12 baby lamb rib chops

Kosher salt, to taste

1. Whisk together the olive oil, vinegar, sugar, mint, and rosemary in a large casserole. Add the lamb chops and rub with the marinade. Allow to marinate at least 30 minutes, and up to overnight.

2. Preheat a grill or grill pan over high heat. Cook the lamb chops for 2 to 3 minutes per side, being sure to develop a char in places. Transfer to a platter, sprinkle with salt, and enjoy.

MARIO
Because I like to go to bed a little on the early side, we ring in the New Year with Rio de Janeiro, which is two hours earlier. So, at ten o'clock we're singing "Auld Lang Syne," and at eleven o'clock I'm in the sack.

Chicken and Chorizo Paella

Serves: **12**   Skill Level: **Moderate**   Prep Time: **15 minutes**   Cook Time: **40 to 45 minutes**

Paella almost always signals that it's "time to party." It's a communal dish that brings everybody together, serving themselves and each other, encouraging conversation, and lingering at the table. Paella can also have seafood in it, but the combination of mild chicken with spicy chorizo is so good, there's no reason to complicate matters with any more ingredients than necessary. The dish is originally from Valencia in Spain, and the word "paella" is used throughout the region as a synonym for "pan"—all kinds of pans. So now you have a little information to share along with this beautiful dinner.

1 tablespoon olive oil

½ pound dried chorizo, sliced in ½-inch slices

4 chicken thighs

4 chicken drumsticks

Salt and freshly ground black pepper, to taste

1 Spanish onion, chopped

2 cups butternut squash, peeled, seeded, and diced small

2 cups uncooked short grain rice

1 teaspoon coriander, toasted and ground

½ teaspoon cumin, toasted and ground

½ teaspoon chipotle powder

¼ cup white wine

5 cups chicken stock

¼ cup cilantro, chopped

¼ cup parsley, chopped

2 jalapeños, seeded, stem removed, and thinly sliced, for garnish

1. In a paella pan or cast-iron skillet, heat the olive oil over medium heat. Add the chorizo and cook until it has rendered its fat and is cooked through. Remove from the pan and set aside.

2. Season your chicken pieces with salt and pepper. To the same pan, add the chicken pieces, skin-side down; brown on both sides. Remove and set aside. Next add the onion and squash to the pan, along with a pinch of salt. Cook, stirring occasionally until the onion is tender and aromatic, about 5 minutes. Next add the rice. Toast the rice with the vegetables for a few minutes, then add the coriander, cumin, and chipotle powder.

3. After about 30 seconds, add the wine, scraping any brown bits off the bottom of the pan, then slowly add the chicken stock. Season again with salt and pepper. Add the chicken pieces back in along with the chorizo, then cover and cook for 15 to 20 minutes, until the rice and chicken are cooked through. Turn the heat off and garnish with the cilantro, parsley, and jalapeños sprinkled over the top. Serve warm.

Tejeringos

Serves: **12**   Skill Level: **Moderate**   Prep Time: **20 minutes**   Cook Time: **10 to 15 minutes**

We say doughnut, but in Mexico they say churro, and in Spain fried, sweetened dough is *tejeringo*. At the end of the day, there's one dessert that everyone loves and that dessert is the doughnut (so there's a version of it in almost every country). We think of doughnuts as something that you go to a store to buy because they seem pretty complicated to make. Not the case at all. These *tejeringos* are amazingly simple to make and also amazingly addictive. So get ready to stand next to the stove for a while. Your guests and family aren't going to let you stop making these until the last bits of batter are gone.

1 cup water

8 tablespoons unsalted butter, cut into 8 pieces

1 tablespoon sugar, plus about 1 cup for dusting

Pinch of salt

1 cup all-purpose flour

3 large eggs

8 cups extra-virgin olive oil, for deep-frying

1 cup bittersweet chocolate, chopped and melted

1. Combine the water, butter, sugar, and salt in a small heavy saucepan and bring to a boil, stirring occasionally until butter melts. Turn the heat to low, add the flour (in one shot), and stir vigorously until the mixture forms a ball. Remove from the heat and add the eggs one at a time, stirring constantly. Transfer to a bowl and allow the batter to rest for 10 minutes in the refrigerator.

2. Meanwhile, heat 3 inches of olive oil to 365°F in a large heavy pot. Transfer the dough to a pastry bag fitted with a large star tip. Pipe 4-inch-long strips of dough into the hot oil, without crowding, and cook for 4 to 5 minutes until golden brown. Drain on paper towels, and repeat with the remaining batter.

3. Dust generously with sugar and serve. Serve with melted bittersweet chocolate if you want!

DAPHNE
New Year's Eve in my family is a big Italian feast, and then a huge sundae bar. All the kids get to eat whatever they want and it's total sugar craziness.

PARTY PLAYLISTS

Every celebration needs a great soundtrack. Music can set the mood, inspire guests to dance, or even spark a sing-along ("Summer Nights" from *Grease*, anyone?). Try to choose songs that fit the theme of your party: if you're having a mellow evening with finger food and cocktails, you might want to go with jazz or R&B. If you're throwing a Halloween party, don't forget to add Michael Jackson's "Thriller" and Warren Zevon's "Werewolves of London" to your playlist. And if you're hosting a rockin' dance party, put up the disco ball, throw on some bell-bottoms, and break out your ABBA, Donna Summer, and Village People records, er, MP3s. Here are some playlists that include our favorite party songs.

MARIO

In Memory of Elizabeth Reed
The Allman Brothers Band

Kashmir
Led Zeppelin

Blue Suede Shoes
Elvis Presley

Where Is the Love?
The Black Eyed Peas

A Love Supreme
John Coltrane

All Along the Watchtower
Jimi Hendrix

Drunk in Love
Beyoncé

Lost in the World
Kanye West

Helter Skelter
The Beatles

Seven Nation Army
The White Stripes

MICHAEL

Good Hearted Woman
Waylon Jennings and
Willie Nelson

Family Tradition
Hank Williams, Jr.

Love Walks In
Van Halen

Jammin' Me
Tom Petty and the
Heartbreakers

Come As You Are
Nirvana

Lovin', Touchin', Squeezin'
Journey

Harvest Moon
Neil Young

Ashes to Ashes
David Bowie

Nightswimming
R.E.M.

All Along the Watchtower
Bob Dylan

All My Mistakes
The Avett Brothers

Cigarettes, Wedding Bands
Band of Horses

Talihina Sky
Kings of Leon

CARLA

Green Onions
Booker T. & the M.G.s

Happy
Pharrell Williams

Mustang Sally
Wilson Pickett

Tightrope
Janelle Monáe

Set It Off
Strafe

Golden
Jill Scott

Pontoon
Little Big Town

DAPHNE

I Knew You Were Trouble
Taylor Swift

We Found Love
Rihanna

Dark Horse
Katy Perry

Drunk in Love
Beyoncé

All of the Lights
Kanye West

Royals
Lorde

One More Night
Maroon 5

SexyBack
Justin Timberlake

Started From the Bottom
Drake

We Can't Stop
Miley Cyrus

CLINTON

The Girl from Ipanema
Astrud Gilberto

Shame, Shame, Shame
Shirley & Company

Ring My Bell
Anita Ward

Never Gonna Give You Up
Rick Astley

Band of Gold
Freda Payne

Baby Got Back
Sir Mix-a-Lot

The Humpty Dance
Digital Underground

Groove Is in the Heart
Deee-Lite

Love Hangover
Diana Ross

INDEX